•What makes the Montessori Method different?

•Are all schools that call themselves Montessori genuine?

•What is the role of the teacher in Montessori?

•Does Montessori stifle a child's creativity?

•Has Montessori been proven effective by test results?

•Does Montessori work only for middle-class children?

•Is the Method too rigid?

•Is Montessori too expensive to be practical?

These are just a few of the vast array of questions that are fairly and fully answered in—

THE ESSENTIAL
MONTESSORI

ELIZABETH G. HAINSTOCK has been actively involved with the Montessori Method since 1960. She received her Montessori certification from the St. Nicholas Training Centre, London. In 1971, she served as Montessori consultant for the Department of Health, Education and Welfare in the formation of its Head Start program, and in 1973 was the recipient of the "Montessorian of the Year" award from the Universal Montessori Teachers Association. She is currently on the board of the International Montessori Society, and continues to give classes and lectures. She is the author of TEACHING MONTESSORI IN THE HOME: THE PRE-SCHOOL YEARS and TEACHING MONTESSORI IN THE HOME: THE SCHOOL YEARS (both available in Plume editions).

THE ESSENTIAL MONTESSORI

Elizabeth G. Hainstock

(God Bless this woman!)

Updated Edition

The Essential Montessori was previously published in a Mentor edition.

REGISTERED TRADEMARK—MARCA REGISTRADA

Library of Congress Cataloging-in-Publication Data

Hainstock, Elizabeth G.
  The essential Montessori.

  1. Montessori method of education.   I. Title.
LB775.M8H26   1986   371.3'92   85-29880
ISBN 0-452-26484-7

First Plume Printing, May, 1986

4   5   6   7   8   9   10   11

PRINTED IN THE UNITED STATES OF AMERICA

For Bill, with love and appreciation

In order to educate, it is essential to know those who are to be educated.

—Maria Montessori,
A Pedagogical Anthropology

Contents

Preface

WHEN THE MONTESSORI method re-emerged on the education scene in the early 1960s, there was, predictably, a great surge of interest and excitement. Its impact was seen and felt in every area of education, to varying degrees and with varying results. This rapid growth of the movement caused it to be looked on by many as a "fad" that would vanish as quickly as it had appeared. Hundreds of articles, books, and talks touted this "new" method of education. The obvious question was "Will it last?" The answer some twenty-five years later is an emphatic "Yes." Not only has Montessori endured, it has also quickly ceased being merely a new phenomenon and has become a viable and established alternative and supplement to more traditional learning practices.

Montessori is a timeless method, with much to offer in the areas of education, child development, and human understanding. Each year brings new teachers and parents curious about how to adapt Montessori to fill their particular needs and interests. It was for this perpetual stream of "newcomers to Montessori" that this book was originally written, and for them also that this current, updated edition is intended. A brief overview of the life on Maria Montessori and the growth and diversification of her method is as necessary now as it was years ago.

This book is not intended to be a scholarly treatise or an encyclopedia of facts about Montessori, nor is it meant to focus on one particular aspect of the method. There is an abundance of books, pamphlets, and other data available on the specifics of the method, as well as lists of "where to find what" (which become obsolete too rapidly to warrant publishing in book form). This book, written for the layperson, is meant to serve as an introductory source for the newcomer to Montessori and as a general review for those already familiar with the method. *The Essential Montessori* condenses and simplifies all that has previously been written about Montessori and acts as a guide to the woman and her method.

-E.G.H.

San Juan Bautista, California
June 1985

THE ESSENTIAL
MONTESSORI

Introduction

TODAY, NEARLY EIGHTY years after the opening of the first Casa dei Bambini in the slums of Rome, interest in the Montessori method continues to spread. Throughout Europe, it has long been an established teaching method, and in many schools, the same principles as used for early education are applied up through high school. In recent years there has also been interest in the method in the world's developing countries.

In the past two decades the method has flourished in the United States. By the mid-1960s the Montessori method was one of the fastest developing and most talked-about phenomena on the American educational scene. Over the years it has been closely examined by and has found support from important leaders in the fields of education and child psychology. Its greatest application has been in the pre-school and primary grades, and its influence has been great. There are now over 3000 schools in the United States that practice some form of the Montessori method. Elements of Maria Montessori's philosophy and materials are used in numerous public school classrooms, in the field of special education, and in federally funded programs such as Head Start and day care centers. The method has proven itself adaptable to all social strata and specialties within the educational spectrum, serving the objectives of many situations and applications.

Dr. Montessori's books have been translated into twenty-two languages and are readily available, usually in both hardcover and paperback editions. Her method has become a part of every teacher-training course, and there are several hundred such courses specifically concerned with providing the Montessori credentials.

Her ideas on early education were revolutionary at the turn of the century. She advocated pre-school education at a time when no school for children under the age of six existed. In an era when children were to be seen and not heard and the adult had total authority, she felt that the child was possessed of a higher intelligence than the adult. Her stress on early cognitive learning in a prepared environment, directed by a teacher and reality oriented, was completely alien.

My interest in the Montessori method began in 1960 when, as a disillusioned student teacher, I saw everything being done for young children who were quite eager and capable of doing things for themselves. My teaching courses had not even mentioned the name of Maria Montessori, but when I read an article about the revival of her method in the United States, I was immediately attracted by its logical, common-sense approach.

My attempts to pursue this interest further were hampered because Dr. Montessori's original writings had long been out of print and copies were unavailable at local libraries. Finally I found two books in the "dead-book" files, and my pursuit began of what to me was a completely new method of education. Pregnant with my first child, I became even keener, and as I read about the method in the Dottoressa's own words and looked at early photographs of her classrooms and materials, my enthusiasm grew.

When E. M. Standing's book *Maria Montessori: Her Life and Work* was published in 1962, I read it eagerly. In spite of its attitude of worshipful adulation, showered on Dr. Montessori by so many of her followers, it gave a thorough account of her life and method.

In the mid-1960s I had the good fortune to meet the Directress of a Montessori pre-school not far from my home. At the time I was working at home with my two daughters, having adapted Montessori's own classroom materials and lessons to more practical home use. She was interested in my approach to Montessori, and I was thrilled at the chance to see an actual Montessori classroom in action. I worked as a classroom volunteer, finally able to add practical application to my reading.

Later I took a teacher-training course from St. Nicholas Training Centre in London and obtained certification as a Montessori teacher.

With three young daughters, my primary interest was in the

teaching of Montessori in the home. Since there were few schools within reasonable distance and prices were too high for most young parents like myself, I began giving introductory courses for parents and public school teachers to acquaint them with the method. Enthusiasm and interest were overwhelming. So little was really known about the method at that time, and the philosophy underlying it was greatly misunderstood and sometimes misrepresented. Many of Dr. Montessori's books were being reissued, and numerous articles were appearing about the revival of this "magic" approach to education. Unfortunately, the method and the mystique were becoming intertwined.

Montessori's own writings were quite technical and frequently written in an awkward pedagogical jargon. Moreover, some people involved with the method were unwilling to share ideas and fostered an aura of secrecy, implying that only a special few could understand and impart the knowledge of this educational approach. This attitude tainted the method and made people arch their backs whenever it was discussed.

Later, my years of classroom involvement and use of Montessori in Head Start programs made me even more aware of the terrible disservice being done the method by keeping it a mystery to the public. In an attempt to simplify it and share with others what I had found to be a successful and helpful approach to child-rearing and early education, I wrote *Teaching Montessori in the Home*.* When it was published in 1968, I was unprepared for the stir that it created. I had naively violated an educational taboo, opening up to the public what had hitherto been jealously guarded and watched over by a handful of protective caretakers. Until this point, the public had been kept in awe of the things that happened behind the closed doors of the Montessori classroom, where only those specially trained could sprinkle the magic dust.

My involvement with the Montessori method has given me many opportunities. A few of the highlights have been dinner and an evening spent with Maria Montessori's son Mario and his wife

---

*A companion volume, *Teaching Montessori in the Home: The School Years*, was published in 1970, and the original volume was retitled *Teaching Montessori in the Home: The Pre-School Years*. Translated into ten languages, and both now available in paperback editions, these books are still useful guides for home application. (See Selected Bibliography, p. 121.)

at the home of his eldest daughter in Laren, Holland; the pleasure of studying under and working with Margaret Homfray and Phoebe Child, early students and dedicated followers of Montessori who now run the St. Nicholas Training Centre; a chance to reminisce with an elderly lady who had attended Dr. Montessori's first training course in San Francisco and later lived with her in Europe; and an opportunity to talk at length to a student who had attended the first United States Montessori school, which opened in Tarrytown, New York, in 1911. All of these experiences and more have enlarged my knowledge of Montessori—the woman and the method—and, I hope, have helped me to be more objective.

Mario Montessori spoke at length about his mother and his dissatisfaction with the way Americans were using the method. He feels that it is becoming too diluted as it's incorporated and adapted by others, and dislikes the fact that it has fallen into the public domain and is no longer something over which he has total control. All of us who are not A.M.I. (Association Montessori Internationale) trained and blessed are rebels in his eyes.

He felt adamantly that the utopian ideal would be to take children at infancy and raise them in a total Montessori environment.

Maria Montessori's granddaughter spoke of her warmly and told how children always loved her and were attracted to her. She said it had seemed odd to her that, as one who had pursued a career, her grandmother had nonetheless been convinced that a mother's place was in the home, reprimanding her granddaughter for expressing interest in finding some activity that would occasionally take her away from the children. She painted a picture of a very proud, dogmatic, and vain woman whose physical activities were curtailed in later years by her portly size, which prevented her even from climbing the stairs to a second-floor flat to see her great-grandchildren.

More insight was given by Yahn Nienhuis in Holland, who now runs the company begun by his father for manufacturing the high-quality Montessori materials in the early 1900s. He spoke of her as a demanding taskmaster who expected others to jump at her command. The early materials had been handmade by Yahn's father, with such demands put on him that his home life and health were nearly ruined, according to Yahn.

Eugenia Andriano, who until her death at close to ninety ran a small Montessori school in her home in California, always expressed great enthusiasm about La Dottoressa. She had felt directly the magnetism of this woman while studying with her, and still spoke of her with reverence more than fifty years later. She told of pulling off her apron after doing her dinner dishes and running down a San Francisco hill to attend Montessori's class each night. She told marvelous stories about staying in Montessori's home with her, of her huge appetite and great culinary skills, and of her ready humor, quick temper, and ability to "turn on the charm" when it was advantageous. Mrs. Andriano showed me many of the original Montessori materials, including spools of colored silk thread used for the color exercises. She emphasized the Montessori philosophy, in which she believed strongly. When we discussed how Montessori was currently so much in vogue with respect to early learning, she shrugged her shoulders and said, "I've never taught any of my pupils to read. I just give them the tools and they read by themselves when they're ready."

I have been fortunate to be able to travel a great deal as a Montessorian, visiting a variety of Montessori schools throughout the United States and Europe, and lecturing in countries and towns where there were no Montessori schools but great interest in starting them. I have managed to acquire "pen pals" from all over the world—from a young teacher in the Philippines to Americans in rural communities and remote foreign villages who were using my books as a guide to starting Montessori classrooms.

What has always intrigued me is the adaptability of the method. I've taught in a "perfectly equipped" school in an upper socioeconomic community as well as in Head Start programs with the culturally deprived and with children who have learning disabilities. I've seen the method work with both retarded and gifted children, successfully adapted into the public school curriculum as well as into parent-run schools in the United States and New Zealand. I've seen it misused, abused, and used to its optimum; it has withstood many tests. To those who say that Montessori is not for every child, I would say that for every child there is something to be learned from Montessori.

Over the past twenty-five years I have remained enthusiastic about the method, developing from a young, idealistic, somewhat zealous crusader into a more realistic and objective participant. The excitement of watching and taking part in the growth of the movement has been exhilarating, and my experiences as a parent have complimented my involvement with the Montessori method.

My daughters, who acted as my guinea pigs, are now young women. Together we look back on our Montessori experiences as among our happiest hours. Those times gave truth to the adage that the formative years from birth to age six are the most important period in a child's development. The time we spent learning together gave me the chance to work closely with my children, laying the groundwork for a continuing rapport in their later years. I was able to watch each of them develop into unique individuals and to learn infinitely more about them than I would have in any other situation. I feel that their emergence as individuals was more readily apparent to me because of our shared Montessori experiences than it would have been if I'd just given them a cheerful good-bye and sent them off to nursery school each morning.

Two of my three daughters have graduated from college and are settled into careers. The youngest is still a student. From the time that they enterd public school, I could see the distinct advantages their Montessori background had given them. They possessed a self-esteem and confidence unknown to me as a child, and always demonstrated an independence beyond their years. They have always been strongly self-motivated and have had a keen interest in learning. How vividly they remember the day-to-day routine of their early Montessori training is not important. What is important are the resulting benefits and the patterns that training established for them to build upon as they matured. The true value of the Montessori method comes when the child is able to *use* the tools and skills learned in earlier years and, in turn, to share them with others.

Obviously, cultural background, family experiences, environment, and other factors played an important part in my childrens' development. I feel, however, that the Montessori method confirmed many of the things I would have done on my own and gave me guidelines that extended my scope and expectations. Maria Montessori became my Dr. Spock, giving me greater insight into the child than my previous readings in the works of other child-rearing experts or the theoretical training in Montessori had ever provided, and helping me to see my children as individuals. To put her ideas into practice and see them work was a rewarding challenge, when my children were young. I am still reaping those rewards as they become adults.

1. Maria Montessori: The Woman and the Method

WHEN THE CENTENNIAL of Maria Montessori's birth was celebrated in 1970, there was no question that she was a woman ahead of her time. Even by today's standards, she would be considered a feminist. In turn-of-the century Italy, she was indeed a woman apart.

Her early detractors were many. She was severely criticized for forging her way in a man's world, and every conceivable obstacle was placed in her path. Thoroughly feminine in appearance, she nevertheless could compete with any man once her mind was made up. Spurred on by her own inner determination and the theories that she was constantly evolving from her observations of young, developing children, she gave birth to a revolutionary new method of childhood education.

Maria Montessori saw much need for reform in the educational system of her day, and because of this, she was concerned more with change than with tradition. Though recognized as a pedagogue, she had been trained as a clinician and her approach was scientific. Her ideas were formulated after she had laboriously observed the needs of the individual child. Her goal was to develop the whole personality of the child, and her system is based on her strong belief in the spontaneous working of the human intellect. Her three primary principles are observation, individual liberty, and preparation of the environment. These principles and their various practical expressions with children are gradually becoming part of our educational system. Our modern kindergartens use the child-size furniture and many didactic materials first introduced by Montessori. Such current concepts as individualized learning, readiness programs, manipulative learning, ungraded

8

classes, combined age groups, team teaching, and open classrooms reflect many of her early insights. Whether it be in an actual Montessori classroom or in a classroom incorporating her ideas, Maria Montessori has left her mark. Today, her innovative ideas parallel the thinking of behavior-modification experts and constitute the framework for many modern-day educational practices. Though its popularity in this country ebbed for a time, the Montessori method has had an unequaled resurgence and continues to grow in the United States and abroad.

Maria Montessori was born in Chiaravalle, Italy, in 1870, the only child of well-educated, attractive, middle-class parents. Both were strong individuals and firm disciplinarians. Her mother, Renilde, was from an academic family. Highly literate, articulate, and religious, with liberal ideas, she encouraged and supported Maria's pursuit of a career. Maria's own strong religious convictions also had a profound influence on her thinking throughout her life.

Her father, Alessandro Montessori, a former military man and a true gentleman of the era, was a conservative in his thinking, and his daughter was to feel his disapproval often. The family moved frequently during Maria's childhood because of her father's job as a successful government finance official for the tobacco industry. This gave young Maria a chance to further her academic and cultural education in the larger cities of Italy.

Even as a child she demonstrated a strong will and sense of self, as well as a desire for leadership. Not academically competitive in her early years, she still found that learning was easy for her and began excelling, particularly in mathematics. She was studious and relished the challenge of problem-solving.

For her first twelve years, Maria attended schools in the province of Ancona. At the age of thirteen, with the support of her mother overcoming the protests of her father, Maria entered technical school, preliminary to an intended career in engineering.

Refusing to become a teacher, then considered the only acceptable profession for young ladies, she entered the Univeristy of Rome as a student of mathematics, physics, and natural sciences. She became interested in biology and decided to study medicine rather than engineering. Her father disapproved of both pursuits, but nevertheless accompanied her to and from classes each day. It was then considered neither proper nor safe for an attractive young lady to appear alone in public.

Maria found medical school a constant struggle, but she refused to be defeated by the obstacles which she encountered in an all-male field. Propriety dictated that she dissect a cadaver alone, rather than with her male peers, and she often worked in isolation from the rest of her class. She studied pediatrics in her last two years, gradually overcoming the earlier lack of acceptance by her male classmates. Excelling in her oral report, she ranked among the highest in her class in 1896, becoming the first woman to be graduated from the University's school of medicine.

Returning to the University to do research work at the psychiatric clinic, she later joined the staff as a volunteer. Her job was to visit insane asylums in order to select patients for treatment at the clinic. Her special interest was in children, and this led her to study the works of Jean Itard and Edouard Seguin, which she painstakingly translated into Italian for herself. They were to have a profound influence on her theories.

Jean-Marc-Gaspard Itard (1775–1838), a Paris physician at an institution for deaf mutes, had won acclaim for his work with the "Wild Boy of Aveyron." He disagreed with those who felt the boy to be ineducable and set out to teach him. He believed that observation was just as important in education as in the treatment of the sick, and that the mind developed through the actions of the senses. He pursued this belief by experiments with the mentally defective.

Edouard Seguin (1812–1880) became a student of Itard. For him, mental deficiency was a pedagogical rather than a medical problem, and he developed a series of graduated exercises to aid the retarded student's motor development. Eventually he moved to the United States, where he continued his work.

The groundwork for their ideas was laid by Jean-Jacques Rousseau (1712–1778), who believed in training all the child's senses as tools to be used for education. For Rousseau, the key to learning lay within each individual child, and the concrete was always the best place to start.

Johann Pestalozzi, a Swiss follower of Rousseau, felt that the senses should be trained through successive stages of learning by formal exercises, progressing from the simple to the more complex. He became an influential teacher in both Europe and America.

In 1837, the German Friedrich Froebel, who improved on Pestalozzi's ideas by incorporating Rousseau's concepts and adding updated theories of his own, established a school for very young children—a revolutionary step for the times. The school became known as a *Kindergarten*, the concept being that in it children could grow like flowers. The Froebel Society was established to spread this philosophy. Froebel saw play as self-activity which formed a significant part of early childhood. He developed educational toys to stimulate awareness and understood learning to be a series of developmental stages in the process of self-discovery.

Rousseau, Pestalozzi, and Froebel all stressed the innate potential of the child and his ability, given proper guidance and direction, to develop along his own natural lines. Maria Montessori studied the work of these men diligently and was deeply influenced, incorporating their ideas into her own developing and expanding theories. Meanwhile, she was also writing articles, attending conferences, and taking courses in anthropology, philosophy, and psychology. It was from her anthropology professor, Giuseppe Sergi, that she learned the methods of scientific investigation and developed her interest in the importance of the school environment. Sergi was a vocal opponent of the women's movement of the day, who saw it as a threat to the family and believed that education for women should concern itself only with preparing them for their roles as mothers!

In 1900, Dr. Montessori became the director of a practice demonstration school, established by the National League for Retarded Children. With twenty-two students, she now had her first chance to make use of Itard's and Seguin's sensory teaching materials and modify them to her own use. She designed and had manufactured a set of teaching materials based on their principles. When the current care and teaching of the retarded proved ineffective, she set out to experiment with modern applications of prior theories and practical adaptations. Through methodical observations of the children and their individual needs, she worked out the means best suited to teach them. Repeating a specifically prepared exercise seemed more effective than having a child try repeatedly to master a task on his own.

Those children who had previously been abandoned as incapable of learning to function productively began showing the ability to care for themselves. When these retarded children passed exams on a level with normal children, she began questioning the caliber of "normal" education, as Seguin had before her.

Montessori was so successful in her work with these children that she was now recognized as an educator, rather than a physician. Her discoveries were greeted with enthusiasm and praise, but not without some skepticism. Realizing that great results could be obtained by applying these theories to the teaching of normal children, she left her work with the retarded. Maria Montessori now knew where her future lay. She wrote:

> After I had left the school for deficients, I became convinced that similar methods applied to normal children would develop or set free their personality in a marvelous and surprising way. . . . A great faith animated me, and although I did not know that I should ever be able to test the truth of my idea, I gave up every other occupation to deepen and broaden its conception. . . . It was almost as if I prepared myself for an unknown mission.*

She continued to take courses, teach, lecture, and study the science of education, and began publishing professional papers, which were widely read and acclaimed.

Dr. Montessori's chance to work with normal children came in January, 1907, with the opening of the first Casa dei Bambini in a tenement in the San Lorenzo slums of Rome. When the building was offered to Dr. Montessori, the owners hoped that she would provide a place where the children of working mothers could be kept off the streets and thereby reduce vandalism. In the end the children were not only off the streets, they became eager students.

At the school, a prepared environment provided the children with what their homes lacked. Montessori had great respect for her pupils and was constantly learning from them. She gave them

*The Montessori Method, p. 33.

the freedom to explore their new environment and to pick and choose those things with which they wanted to work, thus fostering independence. She made many of her own materials and was constantly experimenting, modifying, and adapting things as the need arose.

The materials for learning were designed to be self-correcting, and the children thrived on the activity involved with learning—so much so that Montessori found the best form of punishment was inactivity! In observing these children, she noticed that after doing a particular activity (exercise), the children continued working with it over and over again, rather than putting it away. They seemed to work for the sake of working, not for reward. She introduced reading and writing only because the illiterate mothers of these children begged her to.

The San Lorenzo project marked a turning point in Maria Montessori's career, which would soon cast her in the role of the world's foremost female educator. By now she had attracted attention and acclaim throughout the world. A constant stream of visitors observed her classrooms and were amazed at the quiet activity within.

As a result of this interest, Dr. Montessori's first training course was given in 1909; out of this came the first statement of her philosophy of education, "The Method of Scientific Pedagogy Applied to the Education of Young Children in the Casa dei Bambini." (This appeared later in an English translation as *The Montessori Method*, the first of many papers and books defining her "method" in detail.) The common sense of her theory is sometimes lost in the flowery rhetoric, repetition, and lofty pedagogical phrases that characterize most of her writings. The florid style was a convention in her time and perhaps was better suited to the Italian language than to less flamboyant English. Her writings, though plentiful, lack overall organization and even though she continually revised them, much is repetitious and often quite verbose. In later years, her combining of the mystical and the methodological makes the content even more difficult to understand.

As word of this amazing young Dr. Montessori and her successful method of childhood education gathered momentum, she decided to devote the rest of her life to spreading the word of the Montessori method, through lectures and teacher-training courses around the world. Lecturing extensively*—never using notes or giving the same course twice—her teaching always reflected her new and ever-developing ideas. These ideas were often centered around one central theme, such as freedom, discipline, etcetera.

By 1912, popular periodicals in Europe and America had spread the word of the Montessori method and schools. The most influential magazine in America at that time was *McClure's Magazine,* which published a series of articles complete with photographs of the Casa dei Bambini.

In 1912, the American writer Dorothy Canfield Fisher, who for several years had observed classes at the Casa dei Bambini, published her first book, *A Montessori Mother*, which simplified the philosophy and appealed to parents.

Private Montessori schools started being established in Europe and the United States. Governments of many countries officially adopted the method in their school systems, and Montessori societies were being established throughout the world.

When the first international teacher-training classes were held in January, 1913, students came to Italy from all over the world. Many of these early students became loyal followers and associates of the Dottoressa, and their names would be linked with hers over the years in the spread of the movement. Among them were Helen Parkhurst, who worked with Montessori in America as a teacher and translator, and later as head of the movement here. She then broke away to develop her own system, the Dalton Plan. Claude Claremont, who also took this first course, was prominent in the movement in England. Anna Maccheroni attended Montessori's earlier lectures at the Univeristy of Rome in 1907 and became a lifelong friend, follower, and biographer; she was in charge of the second Casa dei Bambini, which opened in Milan in 1908. Anne George was Montessori's first American student, and she opened the first Montessori school in the United States, in 1911 in Tarrytown, New York. In 1921, E. M. Standing joined the small cult of Montessori disciples, becoming her collaborator, friend, and official biographer. The movement was to become character-

*Although she understood English, Montessori always spoke in Italian with a translator.

ized by this small, loyal band of followers personally devoted to the Dottoressa and dedicated to the spreading of her method.

Montessori enjoyed traveling with an entourage and being the center of attention wherever she went. Her dominant and awesome presence appeared regal to some and struck others as arrogant. An egotism—belief in herself and in what she had achieved and could achieve—dominated everything she did. This kind of egotism was also apparent in her correspondence with others and in some of her writings. Her magnetism attracted people to her in an almost fanatic, cultish way, and from them she demanded a great deal of time, energy, and a total allegiance to her ideas. Disputes arose easily, and those who had been closest to her could find themselves quickly in disfavor. Some of her most earnest and long-time admirers finally detached themselves from her, finding her dogmatic ways and volatile temperament too stifling. Those who knew her well felt that she lacked the ability to distinguish between those who were sincere and those who simply wanted to ride on her wave.

There were nearly one hundred Montessori schools in the United States by 1913, and the system was a topic of interest and controversy. When the Dottoressa herself arrived in America at the end of that year, this interest was at a high never to be reached again in her lifetime. Montessori had been invited by S. S. McClure, whose magazine had heralded the news of her method, and she was greeted with awe and adulation. From 1913 to 1915 her method was endorsed and backed financially by such luminaries as Alexander Graham Bell and Thomas Edison. She was entertained at the White House and lectured to capacity crowds at Carnegie Hall. Many Americans saw her methods as a vehicle for social reform, but unfortunately, it was not public interest that could guarantee the future of the movement, but rather the reaction of the professional teaching community.

In 1915, the National Educational Association invited Dr. Montessori to return to America to set up a model demonstration classroom, later directed by Helen Parkhurst, at the Panama-Pacific International Exposition in San Francisco, and to give her third international training course. This was followed by another course in Southern California.

The Montessori Educational Association, founded in 1913 by

Mrs. Alexander Graham Bell, with Margaret Woodrow Wilson, the President's daughter, as a trustee was dissolved in 1916. Interest in the method had waned, due to differing educational philosophies in the United States and to the inability to accept change, and the Dottoressa herself left the United States in 1918, never to return.

The years 1914 to 1935 saw the movement flourish throughout Europe, with Dr. Montessori giving lectures and training courses in England, Spain, Australia, and Holland. She had the support over the years of such notables as Queen Margharita of Italy, Sigmund and Anna Freud, Gandhi, Piaget, and, later, Mussolini. In 1919, she gave her first training course in London, a practice that she continued every other year until the outbreak of World War II. In the ensuing years the patttern was the same; she attracted devoted followers and established schools, societies, and training classes throughout Europe. In 1926, she lectured in South America, and in 1929, founded the Association Montessori Internationale (A.M.I.).

Hitler and Mussolini were both interested in the method as adaptable to mass education, a means of creating a new social order through the education of the infant. Montessori was always eager to have people adopt her method, but she did not agree with this particular end result. Those who knew her claimed she was apolitical. Italy was her home, with or without Mussolini, and it was possible then to live under Fascism if you did not openly oppose it. Mussolini became the President of the Montessori Society of Italy, and Montessori schools abounded. By 1934, however, friction had developed between Dr. Montessori and Mussolini's leaders. World War II was to bring many changes to the movement throughout the world.

In 1935, the Montessori method was forbidden in Germany by Nazi police, and by 1936, all of the schools in Italy had also closed. Montessori first went to Barcelona but then fled to England when the Civil War broke out in Spain, arriving in time to preside as President of the fifth International Montessori Congress. When Hitler marched into Vienna in 1938, the existing Montessori schools there were also shut down.

In 1939, at the age of sixty-nine, Montessori arrived in India to establish a training center and begin a course. She was warmly received in this country, where her method had been growing in popularity; her ideas had many parallels with the Theosophy of the Indians. Interned there during the war years as an Italian national, she became closely involved with the people and their culture. Her time in India strongly influenced her, introducing a mystical quality into her thoughts and writings, which was probably better suited to the ways of India than to more rationalist cultures abroad.

The war years caused Montessori to pursue a passionate quest for lasting peace through education. She began to analyze the problems of human and social development, in order to find a way to restructure human society. An underlying theme of her later writings was an educational system which would insure peace through moral reform. The care of infants became a central element in formulating her new ideas, which she wrote about in *The Absorbent Mind* and later books. Many books, usually compiled from the lectures she gave in India, were later published under her name, but it is generally felt that much was lost in transcription and translation, and that her earlier works are a more definitive statement of her ideas.

Loyal followers welcomed her back to London in 1946. In 1947, a Montessori Centre was established there, with former students Margaret Homfray and Phoebe Child in charge. When a disagreement erupted over teacher training, La Dottoressa characteristically withdrew her support of the Centre and the two women. They have continued it to this day as the St. Nicholas Training Centre.

In 1947, Montessori returned to Italy at the invitation of the government to reestablish the movement. She made a last trip to India, and was in San Remo, Italy, in 1949, for the Eighth International Montessori Congress.

Honors continued to be bestowed upon her for her contributions to education and the child. She was nominated three times for the Nobel Peace Prize and was an Italian delegate to the UNESCO conference in Florence, Italy, 1950. The Ninth International Montessori Congress in London, in 1951, and a training course in Austria and lectures in Rome would be her last major activities. Maria Montessori had founded what became an international movement and lived to see herself and her theories acclaimed throughout the world. She died shortly before her eighty-second birthday, on May 6, 1952, of a cerebral hemorrhage. She had been living in Holland and was buried in a Catholic cemetery near the Hague. Her last home, in Amsterdam, was made into a memorial to her and to her work. It is now the headquarters for the A.M.I., which was headed by her son Mario until his death in 1982.

Her legacy lives on through her prolific writings, filled with her seemingly endless intuitive insights into the innate ability of the child and the potential of the school. Her name has become synonymous with innovative and liberating ideas for early childhood education, and in this, her contribution goes beyond the educational system that bears her name.

2. Introduction of the Method into the United States

1912

As QUICKLY AS the Montessori method had burst on the American scene in the early 1900s, it was gone. By 1920, Montessori in the United States had become an historical footnote in the educational archives.

There were several prominent reasons for this. Timing was one of the major factors. Another was that Montessori's early support came not from those fundamentalists who were formulating the new theories of psychology and education, but rather from an elite group of progressives. On closer examination, the Montessori method did not fit the stereotype of current American thinking, and, in the final analysis, people just weren't ready for change.

One of the method's biggest detractors, unfortunately, was William Heard Kilpatrick. A professor at Columbia Univeristy Teacher's College, he was an eloquent and influential voice in education at the time who stressed the social development of children in the classroom rather than cognitive learning. He felt that the teacher should be in total control of the students rather than acting as a mere observer of their self-directed learning, as Montessori advocated. He scoffed at Montessori's stress on sensory education and spontaneous interest as the dynamics for learning; for him, the stimuli had to start outside the child.

In the early 1900s, there was a divergence of educational experiments and viewpoints. Prevalent at the time was Darwin's theory of fixed intelligence; his conservative followers felt that intelligence was predetermined by heredity, and thus early educational experi-

19

ences could not significantly influence later intellectual development. Others felt that sending so young a child to school interfered with the rights of the family. Furthermore, the cost of educating children any earlier was argued to be an unnecessary expense, not only wasteful but harmful.

Nursery schools would not attain popularity until after World War I, and the Froebelian kindergarten controversy was at its peak with opponents trying to break away from the system's rigidity.

Followers of John Dewey, considered the dean of American progressive education, felt that nursery schools should foster conformity with group norms, allow children to act upon their feelings without suppression, and emphasize fantasy play. All of these things were in direct opposition to Montessori's beliefs of more cognitive early learning in a reality-oriented, prepared environment.

Some of the contemporary criticisms appearing in print stated that our country had excellent educators of its own, and that the Montessori method didn't present enough of a challenge to American children. It was also claimed that her didactic materials played too dominant and limiting a role. People questioned a form of education in which the child and the teacher shared the same task.

The failure of the method at this time was also based in part on Dr. Montessori's own insistence that she have total control over everything pertaining to her method: teacher training, written material, etcetera. With a movement that was rapidly encompassing the world, this just wasn't possible. Many of those very people who had worked so hard to promote her method in the United States were soon in her disfavor and lost her support.

1958

Just as Kilpatrick's opposition had a decisive effect on the rapid demise of the Montessori movement in America in the early 1900s, so can Nancy McCormick Rambusch be held responsible for its reintroduction and subsequent flourishing in 1958. Having become interested in the method in the early 1950s, Mrs. Rambusch took the Montessori training course in London and returned to the United States, opening a small school in her home. In 1958, she founded the Whitby School in Connecticut, and with the ensuing publicity and enthusiasm generated by this, the Montessori movement was reborn.

There was nothing haphazard about this second revival. Sensing that the timing was now right, Mrs. Rambusch carefully laid the groundwork for its revival by working with interested people in several fields to find the means best suited for presenting Montessori to an increasingly curious public. A campaign was prepared for the receptive communications media, who were then able to promote this new idea.

A teacher-training program was set up at Whitby, and the American Montessori Society was formed for the purpose of representing Montessori in America, disseminating her ideas, and setting up training programs. Parent study groups and local Montessori societies were formed. Most of the early schools were begun by middle-class parents for their own children.

Nancy McCormick Rambusch's book, *Learning How to Learn: An American Approach to Montessori* (1962), answered the questions of many confused parents, who wanted their children to be less group-oriented and more individualistic.

This time the educational climate was receptive to new ideas. There was an increased demand by laymen and educators for some radical changes in education. In the wake of Sputnik, an America which had complacently thought of itself as number one was shocked into action. The existing educational system was critically challenged and reexamined. Emphasis was now being placed on developing the intellectual abilities of children, on the need for more cognitive training at an earlier age. A vast curriculum reform movement in science and math was underway.

The whole climate was responsive to a new emphasis on early learning and development in an attempt to regain intellectual supremacy. Then, too, teaching children with learning disabilities, both mental and physical, was an idea whose time had finally come. The "culturally deprived" child of the Johnson era was also a problem demanding attention. Head Start programs were springing up everywhere, and it was argued that Montessori's greatest success had been with slum children. Her prepared environment was considered the right antidote for children from deprived backgrounds.

America was looking for a panacea, and the Montessori method seemed as viable as any. Here was a practical and successfully proven way to do what the current theorists espoused. It offered individual teaching, early learning, and behavior modification all rolled into one. Spearheaded by its vocal spokeswoman, the movement to win acceptance for the Montessori method in the United States had begun. A responsive and eager public was waiting.

The initial thrust and enthusiasm were overwhelming. Dr. Montessori's books, long out of print, were republished, and the news media were full of stories on the revival of this all-encompassing method. In an attempt to give the public a brief idea of what the method was, concepts were excerpted out of context, and much was written by people who didn't fully understand the philosophy. This only added to the confusion, rather than alleviating it. There were those who gathered from their reading that the classroom was very structured, while others, reading the same information, thought it was overly permissive. Chaos ensued.

Montessori-type schools of varying standards popped up everywhere, and the waiting lists of students grew. Montessori became a symbol of prestige among parents who were thrilled at the thought of *their* child learning to read and write before his friends. These too-eager parents were more guilty than the crusading Montessorians for permitting the method to be overglamorized, overrated, and oversold. The whole thing took on a P. T. Barnum aura.

Parents became caught up in the novelty and mystique of the Montessori materials, paying little attention to the commitment of philosophy which is at the core of the method. They expected, and in many cases were promised, instant results. While the early learning was what appealed to the parents, Montessori's ultimate goal was to create in the child independence, self-discipline, concentration, motivation, and sensitivity to things around him, and it was to this end that her vast array of materials were developed. ("Things are the best teachers.") Like Seguin and Froebel before her, Montessori's educational toys were taking the place of her philosophy, and people were putting the emphasis on the materials rather than on the ideas they were to serve.

In the academic world there was mixed reaction. Maria Montessori's contribution to education had been barely touched upon in most American teacher-training courses. Not enough was really known about the method to make a fair evaluation, and few knowledgeable Montessorians were available to offer enlightenment.

Few actual Montessori schools would allow visitors, and this, too, added to the mystique and confusion. And still the old controversy raged: were her ideas fifty years behind the times, or had she really been fifty years ahead?

Conventional teachers felt threatened by this "new" method, angry that people seemed to feel that traditional teaching was no longer good enough. After all, it presented an approach completely alien to their mode of teaching—an environment in which the teacher was no longer the focal point.

Many hoped that the Montessori movement was a wave that would recede as rapidly as it had appeared. Others recognized its merit and were open-minded enough to want to learn more.

For the most part, in the early 1960s, the Montessori method was oversold. To some it appeared to be a cult; to others, anathema. The result was that an overeager public, looking for magic, was left confused, angry, and having to face stubborn realities.

The whole movement could have died then, a victim of its own enthusiasts. It is to the credit of a handful of dedicated Montessorians that, despite numerous pitfalls and misconceptions, it is still growing and gathering momentum. There are now over 3000 schools in the United States that practice some form of the Montessori method.

On a tour of schools in the U.S.S.R. with a group of educators in 1970, I visited the Cosmos Pavillion at the Exhibit of Economic Achievement. Lena Gitter, a long-time Montessorian, pointed to the replica of "Sputnik" and said, "This is what started it all!" Indeed, this was what had prompted the revival of the method in the United States. Few of us could have then guessed its full long-range impact in the resurgence of interest.

The growth of the movement in America is still far from assured, however. Montessori—the method and the myth—still has obstacles to overcome.

3. Criticisms of the Method

CRITICISMS OF THE Montessori method have been numerous—some justified, others based on misconceptions. It perhaps should be considered a form of flattery that people cared enough about it at least to discuss and analyze it further, rather than discarding it because it was alien to them. No major contribution in any field is without its flaws and controversies, as well as merits. Such is true of the Montessori method.

Schisms within the ranks began with the Dottoressa herself acting as a divisive force rather than uniting those with the same beliefs and hopes for success. Half a century later, her possessive attitude of "my way is the only way" is still carried on by purists who cling tenaciously to the method as it was, refusing to see what it could be.

The attitudes of these purists have been responsible for keeping Montessori out of the intellectual mainstream of education, driving away many who could have become enthusiastic supporters. Ironically, a similar attitude on Dr. Montessori's part was one of the contributing factors to the movements demise in the United States in the early part of the century. She had always insisted on tight control, fearing that her ideas would be distorted by others. This was a legitimate fear, though unrealistic for something as all-encompassing as the movement had become. Throughout her lifetime she had been adamant that hers was the only valid training course. When she died in 1952, there were very few people with credentials from the A.M.I. to teach the courses.

Thus, a major problem has been with the Montessorians themselves, who have been unable to attain a level of harmony within the system. Not only does everyone involved seem to see and interpret things differently, but there is also an inability to share knowledge and ideas for the benefit of those within as well as outside of the movement. A unified center could greatly extend Montessori's contribution to education today.

As with anything currently in vogue, there are always those who rush to cash in on it. Unfortunately, some schools were opened purely as speculative business ventures; some were franchised. Montessori materials began appearing in many toy catalogs and on classroom shelves where their use and purpose wasn't even understood or known. Visits to several different Montessori schools could provide the visitor with many different views of the method. Montessori had become a generic term, considered to be in the public domain, thereby becoming fair game for those not knowledgeable or trained specifically in the doctrine.

Since the method's reintroduction in the late 1950s, the method has run the risk of being destroyed by those very people who are trying so hard to preserve it. It cannot survive if it is not allowed to keep up with current educational innovations. The fact that the movement has not died in this second revival is a tribute not so much to todays Montessorians as to the innovative ideas of Dr. Montessori herself. Her approach is as viable today as it was seventy years ago. It seems to survive in spite of its proponents, not because of them. Fortunately today's educational community is closer to accepting Montessori on its own merit, and not because of the massive promotional campaigns that have often been waged on its behalf.

Dr. Montessori herself was a paradox in many ways. It is interesting that at the height of her research there were many ideas on child development and education which she simply chose not to delve into. Others she alluded in later writings but never formulated as concrete ideas. She was, in many ways, very narrow and self-serving in her thinking.

It is unfortunate that in the late 1920s, Dr. Montessori began to focus all her energies and attentions on preserving the movement and method, and ceased her research and innovative approach. Ironically, she who had begun as such a methodical observer, aware of the need for change and constant updating, suddenly seemed to feel that her goal had been reached and that there was no further need for improvement and growth. The preservation, acceptance, and universality of her achievement became her new focal point. Her later writings, too, became repetitions of earlier ideas rather than additions to them. Montessori had now become a business, a sacred cow to be preserved intact by a small band of worshipful followers, who zealously guarded their mentor and her method. A few of her more devoted fans later tried to write about her, but it is difficult for the reader to get an objective view when everything is written in such a worshipful and maudlin style. Anna Maccheroni, close to Dr. Montessori for over forty years, entitled her book *Maria Montessori: A True Romance*. E. M. Standing, her later disciple and biographer, used much the same approach in his work *Maria Montessori: Her Life and Work*. These early biographers and followers revered her to the degree that portrayals of her are often less than accurate. Far from being the perfect saint depicted by them, she was a considerably more interesting and complex person. With her best interests at heart, they nonetheless failed to do her justice.

Purists continually have the tendency to credit every innovation in early education exclusively to Dr. Montessori, forgetting that even within the method that bears her name, most ideas were freely adapted from others before her. She herself was an intelligent and eclectic gatherer of many ideas that later became known as "Montessori." It is a shame that so many Montessorians today cannot see the value of being equally open-minded and incorporating new educational ideas.

ANSWERS TO SOME COMMON CRITICISMS

Dr. Montessori had specific reasons for all of her theories and actions, including those that, to some, seem contradictory. I have listed and briefly answered a few of the most common criticisms. Throughout this text, as the reader gains deeper insight into the method, answers to these questions will also become more clearly defined.

The Montessori method deprives children of their childhood by introducing cognitive learning at such an early age.

Evidence clearly shows that the early years, from birth to six, are the most formative and are too often wasted by not realizing the child's true potential. Gradual, sequential learning at this stage can be easy, fun, and important to the developing child. As the sensitive periods show, these early years are when the child learns with the greatest ease and is most responsive to particular phases of learning. To the young child, learning is a natural function of childhood—effortless and challenging, and more meaningful than idle play.

Organizing the way each child is to use a piece of apparatus doesn't allow enough room for imagination, creativity, and spontaneity.

The use of the materials is standardized to help build up concrete patterns of order in the young child's mind. Once this happens, the child is free to work with the materials and use them in other ways. Children experience the spontaneous joy of learning, and each new piece of equipment or new lesson, no matter how standardized, is exciting to the child simply by virtue of its being a different challenge. Once the child begins with the concrete, he is better able to grasp abstract interpretations.

The Montessori classroom doesn't allow enough time for social development and interaction with other children through group activities.

In a Montessori classroom this is quite the contrary. Here the children have far more opportunity for really purposeful interaction because of the prepared environment. There is a great feeling of mutual help and reliance on each other throughout the day, rather than only at specific times. Group activities arise spontaneously throughout the day and may take the form of music and movement exercises, conversation, mealtime, outdoor recreation, or similar activities. In a Montessori classroom the children are thought of as individuals, not as "the group," for respecting each child's individuality finally means less regimentation.

There is not enough emphasis on music, art, and creativity.

Like so many things within the Montessori method, it is quality not quantity that is important. Most Montessori schools present a very distinctive music program as part of the curriculum. This allows the children to learn about music theory, rhythm, and such, not merely walk around making noise with different instruments. Creativity, as such, takes place in every activity with which the child is involved. Art, too, is an integral part of the classroom, but perhaps not as noticeably as in nursery schools where there is a specific time for art and everyone participates, whether they want to or not. Art work, too, is individualized, since it is done when the particular child feels the need. A large variety of materials are available, again giving the child freedom of choice in his medium.

There is not enough fantasy play.

Dr. Montessori felt that it was important for the child to distinguish between fantasy and reality and to know the relative importance of each. She found that young children are more interested in imitating realistic things in their environment. While the Montessori classroom doesn't have a dress-up corner, children are involved with acting out stories and dramas.

The Montessori classroom presents too utilitarian and structured an atmosphere and the materials are too restrictive.

The method itself is not structured, but the approach of many of the teachers is. Although the Montessori method adheres rigidly to the concept of three specific principles, it achieves great flexibility in learning situations. The need for order in the environment of the young developing child was something that Montessori felt should be emphasized, thus "a place for everything and everything in its place" is the way the classroom is arranged. The child relies upon the security of knowing that everything has a place and will always be found there. It is a *prepared* environment, and there is nothing in it that is superfluous to the child's needs. Everything within is something which is needed by the child in his stages of development, and each piece of apparatus serves a specific purpose. It is an environment in which the child functions freely, fulfilling his own inner needs.

There is too much sit-down work.

There is a difference between wandering aimlessly around the room and purposeful activity. Any activity that involves concentration and working with materials will, of necessity, be done sitting down. The distinction here is that the children are not expected to remain rigidly sitting at their desks for lessons, but instead, choose their own materials and work with them where they wish for as long as they wish. Often a single child will be sitting at a table working, or with a group, or working on a mat on the floor. It is not uncommon to see a child with a project spread out before him suddenly get up and go outside to play, then come back and resume his work.

Too much free choice is confusing to the young child and there is too much freedom in the classroom.

It is by individual free choice that the child perfects himself and is enabled to work with the particular piece of apparatus most needed to fulfill something within him. It would be far more confusing to him if there was a large choice of items whose purpose he didn't understand. Instead, these materials are all familiar to him, and consequently he has greater respect for them as learning tools. The freedom within the Montessori classroom enables the child to move about at will, but with respect for others as his guideline.

There is too much emphasis on "practical life" exercises.

This is done purposely to take advantage of the child's desire to imitate things that he sees around him and to help him learn to function in his own environment. More important, each exercise is a potential occasion for the concentrated activity associated with "normalization" and is preliminary to more advanced learning. It is here that the child gains experience, through sensory exercises, in eye-hand control and coordination, small and large muscle control, and coordination and dexterity and refinement of skills needed for later reading and writing. Early sensorial activities lay the foundation for later intellectual activity.

There is too wide a range of age grouping within each classroom.

Montessori felt that the children were far less inhibited when learning from their peers. There is much that a child can teach another child more easily than a teacher can. There is mutual respect among the children and a lack of competitiveness that allows them to learn from each other. It is an ungraded classroom with emphasis on individuals rather than age.

The expense of a Montessori school is not warranted for early education.

A Montessori school is no more expensive than any other form of education. Our society has been geared to thinking of money being put away for a child's *college* education, but too few realize that the early years are crucial for all later learning, and that therefore the cost would seem warranted.

It is a method mainly for the upper class, who would learn with or without Montessori.

Upper-class children may begin the method with some advantage, but children from all socioeconomic strata benefit from it, because it helps to set good learning patterns for future academic achievement. Montessori is not mainly for the upper class, and has been used with great success in all areas of education. There are many public school programs utilizing the method.

There is a lack of conclusive studies showing the advantage of a Montessori education.

This, unfortunately, is true, but the importance of an early Montessori education is in the habit patterns that are built up within the child at a crucially sensitive period, which hopefully would be supported and encouraged in later years. These "lifelong" attitudes include an organized approach to academic skills and problem-solving and the development of independence, self-discipline, and self-esteem.

Will the child with a Montessori background be able to adjust socially and academically to his peers in public school?

This is a very valid question and one that many have studied. Much depends on the quality of the school and the teacher, both Montessori and public. The child, however, will arrive at any school eager to learn and everything will be different, which in itself is a challenge that the child enjoys. Socially he will adjust well because he is used to working closely with his peers and sharing ideas with them. He will normally be more independent than his non-Montessori peers and thus able to do well on his own. Some students will become restless with the teacher-dominated classrooms, the rigidity of desks, and routine. More often, the child adjusts well.

There is much variation among Montessori teachers and schools. The name "Montessori" doesn't seem to mean that they're all the same.

Because the term "Montessori" is considered generic and in the public domain, there are often unqualified people using the name for their schools. This is why it is important to research a school and its staff before becoming involved. Though in practice even accredited Montessori schools can differ in applying the doctrine, they still share a common philosophy based on three primary principles: early childhood, the learning environment, and the role of the teacher. Even though training courses are somewhat alike in theory and external form, there may be considerable differences in actual practice and interpretation in each classroom. Interestingly enough, it is this very individuality which Dr. Montessori felt to be so important that causes independent interpretations in her teachers today. This sometimes leads to misunderstanding as to why the method isn't totally uniform in application. There will always be those who prefer to adhere strictly to what Maria Montessori set forth in principle but unwittingly fail to follow through in actual practice. There will also always be those who see the method as only a vague, imprecise, and limited philosophy to be adapted to their own needs and ideas.

The method is outdated and not current with today's educational theories.

Many of Montessori's ideas have already been incorporated into today's educational programs so that the method obviously has benefits. On the other hand, too often people automatically assume that if something has been around for a while it must be outdated. The very fact that the method has endured for seventy years gives it a kind of validity. In many cases, educators and behaviorists are just now catching up with Montessori!

How can it be useful to normal children when it was originally developed for defectives?

Because of the method's great success with the deficients with whom Montessori originally worked, she decided that there must be something lacking in the education of normal children, and therefore it was to this group that she shifted her emphasis. Over the years, by adaptation, the method has come to be used for education in *all* categories of learning.

4. Adaptability of the Method

ALTHOUGH IT WAS Dr. Montessori's intention that her philosophy and method be applied throughout the entire education of the child, there are few Montessori programs in the United States today beyond the third grade, and the popular concept of the method is in relation to a primary program for children aged 2–6. One of the early stigmas that still persists is that the method is tied to the image of a suburban white middle- and upper-class educational system. Actually these children are no less in need of Montessori's "normalizing" environment than those from more economically disadvantaged circumstances. With the Montessori method, however, they have the added advantage of the long-range attitudes taught within the system.

Today there are an increasing number of Montessori programs for children of diverse racial, ethnic, and socio-economic backgrounds, as well as for the disadvantaged and special child (i.e., gifted, retarded, physically handicapped, emotionally disturbed). It is well suited to an egalitarian society and the complex needs inherent in today's metropolitan communities, because it deals with each child as an individual striving to fill his own particular needs.

Large numbers of children can be taught in the Montessori classroom because most of the children are involved in their own projects or working with others at something. The teacher is freed to act as a director of their spontaneous learning. It differs, too, from conventional group-oriented and subject-matter-oriented educational systems by being a system of human development through individualized learning, and for this reason can be used in a variety of situations.

SPECIAL EDUCATION

Montessori provides a responsive environment to those with special needs, and its adaptation has long been found useful by teachers in all areas of special education. These teachers, like Montessori before them, must be innovative, experimental observers of children with a wide range of physical, emotional, social, and intellectual disabilities. Because of the emphasis on individual needs and the use of sensorial didactic materials, the method is easily suited to change and adaptation to individual needs and levels of learning. Strong sensory stimulants are needed to attract the attention of defective children. The materials are designed so that, used in the proper sequence, they lead the child gradually into an understanding of abstract ideas. This sensori-motor approach to learning is especially effective in special education. Here is an opportunity to learn through exploration and repetition while proceeding at the child's own pace. The child with special needs often becomes confused and overly excited when confronted with the varied materials available in the Montessori classroom and naturally, modification to each situation is needed.

I once taught in a classroom of "normal" children which also included three children with varying degrees and types of learning disabilities. I was amazed at how easily these three appeared to become "normalized" when freed from the pressures that they had encountered in non-Montessori classrooms. Now they were allowed to work by themselves or in a group, to work uninterrupted, at their own pace, under no time pressure, and now, finally, to *succeed* in their endeavors.

Among my numerous correspondents over the years have been two that continue to bring me particular pleasure and a reaffirmation of the contribution and versatility of this method. One, in Virginia, is the mother of a mongoloid child doomed to achieve at only minimal level. We have talked by telephone and exchanged letters for nearly eight years, and the progress in her daughter has elated the parents and astounded physicians. The other is the mother of a brain-damaged son who had not been helped through the normal patterning programs. Both these mothers began a simplified "at home" program with their children, starting at the very beginning by reinforcing the most basic skills. With immense patience, they have worked up to a level that neither thought obtainable.

The possibilities for Montessori in all areas of special education hold an even greater potential, given more study, research, and knowledge of adaptabilities.

CULTURALLY DISADVANTAGED

The greatest beneficiaries of Montessori education are the culturally disadvantaged children, particularly in the inner city. Montessori was concerned with social problems all of her life, and her greatest success has been with slum children. Yet today, though it is used in Head Start, Home Start and disadvantaged programs, it is not as widespread as one might expect and hope. Its use in these programs has been most successful, with the enrichment provided by the prepared environment being a particular antidote for children from "culturally disadvantaged" backgrounds.

Interestingly, the thing most readily noted when working with the disadvantaged is that whereas they may sometimes lack the home stimuli that lead to the greater intellectual prowess of their upper-class peers, they are leaps ahead of them in the exercises of practical life and taking care of their own needs. These things have been self-taught out of necessity.

BEHAVIOR MODIFICATION

Montessori's compatibility with what current behavioral scientists and educators are finding out about early education is significant. They feel a necessity to develop certain habit patterns through carefully planned learning programs. Their studies also show that children learn best in an atmosphere of freedom with clearly defined guidelines. Behaviorists' studies have shown conclusively that children desire to learn and do not need to be motivated by reward and punishment, and, more importantly, that the preschool child is indeed ready for cognitive experiences. They feel that a challenging early environment leads to better, and, ultimately, higher rates of intellectual development; the senses play an imporant part in intellectual development, and children do indeed have sensitive periods.

PUBLIC SCHOOLS

The impact of Montessori education in the public sector has continued to grow, since the establishment in 1965 of the first Montessori public elementary school in Cincinnati. I myself have worked in pilot programs on the West Coast, and have seen Montessori materials correctly and effectively used by teachers unaware that they were using Montessori materials! It is impossible to obtain accurate estimates of the number of public schools that use Montessori materials, especially because schools often use the materials without fanfare, in order to avoid possible controversy. But today's educational climate is more conducive to innovative approaches, and the Montessori method is being incorporated into more school curriculums.

Educational administrators have been reluctant to develop Montessori programs because they are required to hire certified teachers who have completed a traditional four-year education course. The public school classrooms now using Montessori are those conducted by teachers who have adapted Montessori for their own uses. The materials make a classroom look "Montessori," but the teachers do not usually follow the Montessori technique and philosophy.

Many public agencies and the Montessori community at large would like to see the method firmly implemented in public classrooms. Hopefully, a plan can be implemented whereby public schools throughout the United States will hire Montessori teachers who qualify for a special Montessori teacher certification under standards by the I.M.S.

IN THE HOME

The home, which is the child's first learning environment, is the ideal place to begin Montessori, and the mother is the most logical first teacher for the child. It is she who is most interested in his well-being and spends the greatest amount of time with him in his early, formative years. Her influence on the young child is strong.

To actually take the time to work with your child gives you the excitement of seeing him develop as a thinking individual. His "explosion into learning" comes about with your help. The home environment is a natural source of learning and discovery for the child. By scaling things to his size and making things more easily accessible to him, you will greatly facilitate his learning to help himself function on his own in this environment.

Montessori-type materials can be made easily by using and adapting things that are commonly found around the home, and the lessons too are readily adaptable. For those who cannot afford to find a good Montessori school, teaching Montessori in the home can be a successful and rewarding experience.*

FEDERALLY FUNDED PROGRAMS

The method has long been used in Head Start programs, but not to the extent that one would hope. In 1972, a new program was initiated by the Office of Child Development. Called Home Start, and meant to precede the Head Start programs, it was intended as a home-based program for disadvantaged pre-school children and their families, and proposed an alternative way of providing a Head Start-type program for young children in their own homes. Its objectives were to involve parents directly in the educational development of their children and help them to help their children. This program utilized the community, and was to be flexible and sensitive to ethnic, cultural, and local needs. The major focus was on the parent as the first and most influential teacher. The author served as a Montessori consultant and resource person on the founding committee, and was pleased at the route the program attempted to take. However, it has not been as successful as originally hoped.

Day care centers too have made use of the method, but once again, not to the extent Montessorians have hoped for. Federally

*Teaching Montessori in the Home: The Pre-School Years and Teaching Montessori in the Home: The School Years both books by Elizabeth Hainstock, published by New American Library.)

funded programs have not been really successful, due to the lack of trained personnel. Time and costs involved in Montessori training are the prime factors for this. With more study and more qualified Montessori teachers available for these programs a great need could be filled. Presently, many teachers involved in these federally funded programs are using such texts as *Teaching Montessori in the Home* and attending local Montessori workshops to learn how to adapt the method to their own needs.

In the early 1970s A.M.S. worked to implement a mandate received from H.E.W.'s Advisory Committee to assume leadership in developing an Early Childhood Education "umbrella" organization for teacher training accreditation criteria. This would include early childhood training organizations other than Montessori and would involve children from infancy to 12 years.

In 1984, I.M.S. submitted a proposal to HEW recommending revision of federal day care regulations to exempt, at the request of state agencies, Montessori's schools from complying with certain requirements. The main purpose of the proposed revision is to allow Montessori schools not complying with inappropriate day care regulations to still participate in federally funded programs, and thus allow the development and growth of Montessori schools in poorer communities, where they are especially needed and beneficial.

5. The Relevance of Montessori Today and in the Future

MANY PEOPLE QUESTION whether a method devised over seventy years ago can be relevant today. I say yes. There is little that is totally "new" today. Moreover, "new" doesn't always connote "good." Too often we forget that in education today, overlooking proven methods for more modern, seemingly innovative ideas that sometimes do not withstand the test of time.

The Montessori method was conceived as an indirect approach to learning, presenting a comprehensive view of the child. Montessori regarded the classroom as a laboratory for observing children and testing and retesting ideas and aids to their growth. She approached education as a scientist and pursued her ideas with an open mind, always with strong respect for the child as an individual. It was a scientifically designed method to develop the whole personality of the child at his own natural rate of progress, and thus free his potential for self-development within a prepared environment.

Montessori felt that for each of the four stages of human development (birth to six, six to twelve, twelve to eighteen, and eighteen to twenty-four) it was necessary to change our basic approach to the child, not just give him harder work.

The Montessori curriculum places no restraints on the student's ability and provides manual and physical activity through use of concrete and abstract experiences to help him gain mastery of himself and his environment. The materials allow the child to explore the world through his various senses. Lessons allow him to gain self-confidence and self-mastery—knowing how to do things for himself—through the successful completion of work that is meaningful to him. He gains the confidence necessary to competence by experiencing only temporary failures as he works from the simple to the more complex. Dr. Montessori felt that self-education was of the greatest value and that to be in control of one's self the ultimate achievement.

What has always been most unique about the Montessori method is the detailed emphasis given to sensorial experiences, and herein lies the key to its great success in later learning.

In working at home with my daughters, and in programs with the culturally deprived, the advantages of the early sensorial experiences were constantly reaffirmed. These exercises provide the child with greater powers of discrimination, observation, awareness, control, coordination, and judgment. He becomes a careful observer by working within the method and comes to better understand the realities of life and how to cope with them. He develops pride in himself through success and the self-mastery that allows him to do things for himself. Good study patterns are formed, as well as positive attitudes toward work and learning. Used correctly, the method gives the child a wonderful preparation for life and makes him better equipped for survival in today's world.

The world today has become so fast-paced and competitive that it is more important than ever for our children to emerge as self-reliant, intelligent, motivated individuals who will fully develop their potential. It's vital now to teach children *how* to learn, since we now know that by nature they *want* to learn. More than any other approach, the Montessori method takes into account the whole child and his place in the community. There is a balance inherent in the application of the philosophy that provides for the total development of each child.

We must remember Montessori's admonition, to observe and take our leads from the child. American teachers too often seem to have great difficulty in understanding that the motivation for learning comes from within the child and cannot simply be taught. The person who goes into teaching in order to control others will feel threatened by this method and should not be a part of it. Because of the feeling for the child as creator of the man, and the role of the teacher as mainly an observer, it is important for a good teacher to understand the philosophy behind the method. The good Montessori teacher is less concerned with academic achievement than with those preliminary steps that lay the foundation for it. Though early reading and writing appeal to many parents, these are actually the natural by-products of the other preliminary activities.

Montessori felt that nursery schools should foster self-reliance and independence, and be reality oriented. It is in reviewing Montessori's ideas that we can see its place in education for today and the future.

If Montessori is to continue to be beneficial, people must overcome their undue emphasis on the materials and not be so obsessed and fascinated by them that they forget their relative position within the method. The materials are not magic and do not, by themselves, provide an environment responsive to the needs of the young child. The Montessori philosophy is the most important ingredient in this method, with the materials serving only as tools for its implementation.

If Montessori is to be relevant today, we must remember that it is a method based on observing the child and creating new ideas to aid his development. We must continue to work on this premise today and thus update Montessori classrooms. We must take into account changes in concepts of psychological development and changes in our culture if we are to respond to the needs of the child. As originally conceived, the Montessori method must not be a stopping point, but rather a springboard for new ideas embracing today's world and today's children. The Americanization of Montessori has added easels, clay, and modern educational materials to the classroom. This has created a split in the movement, with the more rigid followers still using only the original Montessori materials rather than adapting and changing with the times.

I have continually locked horns with the priests, who won't open themselves up to ongoing changes in education but cling to Montessori's early practices as gospel. I feel that if the method is to be a viable element and hold its rightful place in education today, it must be integrated, supplemented, and revised. Montessori is not the only way; it is one of many. To do the best by our children, we must analyze and study them all, and not be afraid to be eclectic. This is the only way in which we can be truly successful and effective in educating for the world of today and tomorrow.

The most positive effect the Montessori method has had is to make open-minded professionals and parents alike take stock of the merits of traditional schooling. Montessori proved to be a method adaptable to many learning situations by presenting such a commonsense "natural" approach to learning. Here was a philosophy that allowed the child to develop naturally and spontaneously, according to his individual needs, to, in fact, teach himself, by using his eyes, hands, and mind together.

As times and ideas have changed and advanced, so too have there been changes within the worldwide Montessori community in the decades since La Dottoressa's death. The true spirit of her work is sometimes forgotten as people are caught up in the surface, rather than the substance of her teaching. Superficially, Montessori is a combination of things which have become synonomous with the name (i.e., prepared environment, materials, freedom, etc.). Add to this the fact that "Montessori" has, since 1967, been deemed a generic term, and justifiable confusion arises. Because of these and other factors, the name Montessori has been brought to the forefront of education, while ironically loosing much of its own true identity in the process.

A.M.S. and A.M.I were the acknowledged standard-bearers in the years following the method's reintroduction into the United States. There was much feuding between the two organizations however, as often happens in such situations. The leaders of the two groups often seemed to be more concerned with defending their own turf than in reaching out to the world at large. A new challenge was needed to remind them of their proper role. This came in 1979 with the formation of the International Montessori Society.

The I.M.S. has answered the question "What is Montessori?" by restating Dr. Montessori's fundamental vision of a "new education" that will assure the emergence of the "normalized" child in the world. It believes that the three basic principles of observation, individual liberty, and preparation of the environment constitute the complete (essential) basis of Montessori, and that conscious awareness of them will result in the "completion" of Montessori education. The reason for establishing the Society was to communicate this message to others.

Currently Monessori schools are governed by the same requirements for licensing set forth for operation of day care centers. On a statewide basis this has increasingly posed problems to the regulating of Montessori schools. Local agencies have sought to impose rigid provisions for licensing. Most states even go so far as to specify classroom materials, teacher/child ratio, maximum group size, minimum space requirements, and specific teacher qualifications.

The I.M.S., in an attempt to preserve and advance Montessori, has actively, although not always successfully, sought individual state waivers of detrimental regulations and encouraged the establishment of legitimate standards for genuine Montessori schools. As a Society it also offers its members assistance and support regarding government regulations and the operation of individual Montessori educational programs.

Most prominent of the I.M.S. court challenges is one continuing in the state of Maryland, filed in 1981. This case, in which the Society claims a denial of constitutional rights in the operation of private education and academic content censorship, is currently under appeal. It is a sad commentary on education in a free democracy that such an action needs to be taken at all. Cases like this have become a necessity as Montessori schools seeking to implement true Montessori principles have faced government hostility in the enforcement of licensing. Government agencies must increase their awareness of Montessori and recognize the unique and separate character of Montessori schools versus regular day care schools.

An added dimension is an increasing interest in further expansion of Montessori into the elementary years. This expansion would be a natural continuation of the philosophy and fundamentals of "normalization" already established. It would also lead to a cohesiveness in the child's development that is often lacking in the transition to a more traditional education. Naturally the prepared environment would have to be modified to correspond with the broader interests and more diverse areas of study for the other child. Although required curriculum of elementary education limits the child's freedom, each child can still march to the beat of his or her own drum within given parameters. Montessori-style elementary education would be based on the belief that the child who enjoys learning and is allowed the freedom to pursue his interests tends to improve automatically and master his math and language skills, as he sees perfecting these tools as a means to achieve his own ends.

The greatest drawback to the success of such a program is the lack of properly trained teachers. The skills and training needed to create an appropriate learning environment for the child from six to twelve demand an advanced knowledge of technique as well as the ability to let the child pursue his natural course of development. Traditionally trained elementary teachers may often defeat this unique purpose of Montessori education and severely impede the child's attempt to "normalization."

The most effective elementary program would require training Montessori primary teachers or training young teachers specifically for Montessori elementary teaching. Dr. Montessori herself believed that a "new education" would emerge when the adult's prejudices about the child were removed. Thus an educator, truly committed to the principles, must free himself of the restrictions of traditional education, where he has been the dominant force, at times even the obstacle to the child's development. Creating this "new education" is a total commitment, beginning with the proper training and certification of effective Montessori teachers able to implement the program. Success in the continuation of the Montessori method on a higher level is yet to come.

The future direction of the method is anybody's guess, given the continuing experiments and changing trends in education and the fickleness of the public, which always wants what is "in" rather than what has proven itself. Montessori has unquestionably established that in education at the present time, and gives every indication of maintaining its position and growing stronger.

I feel that in the next decade we will see more schools incorporating Montessori's ideas and materials and fewer "pure" Montessori classrooms. So many "Montessori-like" materials are in all the catalogs now that its hard to remember that in the early 1960s "learning toys," as we know them, did not exist. As for the future, certainly Montessori's philosophy and today's "high tech" learning devices complement each other in the classroom. La Dottoressa's philosophy and materials will continue to serve as the core, with her method becoming a part of an eclectic educational picture rather than something set apart as unique and exclusive. Maria Montessori will then take her rightful place among the great educators and innovators of our time, rather than as the leader of a cult.

6. Montessori's Views of Her Work

IN PRESENTING DR. Montessori's works, I have chosen to rely on her own words.* I feel that it is more important for the reader to read selections from her own writings and thus gain the flavor of her style, than it is to impose my own interpretations. I have also chosen those selections that convey her message in simple pedagogical language. I hope this will serve as an adequate condensation of her philosophy and insights for those who would not ordinarily choose to read her major works in their entirety.

It is my hope that these direct quotes from her writings, grouped together under related headings, to express her ideas, will tempt the reader to research more fully the particular aspects which interest him. The culling of general ideas from a thick mass of pedagogical confusion will, I think, make the reading of the Montessori philsophy easier and more enjoyable.

The Absorbent Mind	AM
The Montessori Method	MM
The Discovery of the Child	D
The Secret of Childhood	S
From Childhood to Adolescence	C–A
Dr. Montessori's Own Handbook	H
Spontaneous Activity in Education	SAE
Childhood Education	CE

*Code for books used for quotations. All references are to editions listed in Selected Bibliography, pp. 121–127.

THE FIRST CHILDREN'S HOUSE

The environment in which the first Children's Houses had their origins must have been extremely favorable, since the surprising results obtained during those first years have never again been equaled . . . the people . . . were poor, honest, but without any particular profession. They lived from day to day on chance work . . . They lived surrounded by people who were coarse and immoral. And all of these unfortunates housed in the rebuilt apartments were without exception illiterate. The children worked together in a kind of common paradise. Because of their parents' ignorance they received no education from their families. Neither were they influenced by the ordinary type of education that children receive in school. The mistress in the first Children's House was not a real teacher, but a woman with only a small amount of education who had worked as a domestic and had labored in the fields farmed by her family. She had no ideas about teaching, no principles of education. . . . During the day the children were abandoned by their fathers and mothers as they went out in search of work. These circumstances, which might seem to preclude any favorable outcome for a school, proved to be a necessary condition. They created a neutral atmosphere as far as any educational influence was concerned. The work of the school proceeded in a truly scientific fashion since it was not opposed by any obstacles. And this freedom from any hindrances contributed much to the happy outcome of the experiment. The Children's House was thus a kind of psychological laboratory, unharmed by any prejudices . . . It was precisely this group of raw and unkempt children that became a famous center of interest, drawing visitors from all parts of the world, and particularly from the United States, as if to an educational Mecca . . . The history of the movement shows that the same kind of education, though with some adaptations, is applicable to all grades of society, and to all nations of the world, and it may be used with children from happy homes as well as with those who have been terrified by earthquake or some similar disaster. . . . The Children's House has a twofold importance. It is socially important in that it is a "school within a house." It is educationally important, but its success here depends upon the application of the method which I learned through experience. (D, 38–41)

As soon as I realized that I had a school for small children at my disposal, I decided to make a scientific study of their education and strike out on a new path . . . The new type of education, which I hoped to introduce, was . . . based on objective research which, it was hoped, would "transform the school" and act immediately upon the pupils, inspiring them with a new life . . . My intention was to keep in touch with the research of others, but to preserve my own independence. (D, 42–43)

SOURCES OF INSPIRATION

Montessori openly acknowledged her indebtedness to others and freely credited them with the part they played in the formulation of her own ideas. Just as those who have succeeded her have borrowed and interpreted freely from what has become known as "Montessori," so too did she have her sources of inspiration.

It is a credit to her inquiring mind and determination that she so methodically sought to study every aspect of her chosen field and to look to those who had come before her for guidance and the foundation for newer and updated ideas.

I followed Seguin's book, and also derived much help from the remarkable experiments of Itard. Guided by the work of these two men, I had manufactured a great variety of didactic material. These materials . . . became, in the hands of those who knew how to apply them, a most remarkable and efficient means. . . . (MM, 36)

. . . I translated into Italian and copied out with my own hand, the writings of these men, from beginning to end . . . I chose to do this by hand, in order that I might have time to weigh the sense of each word, and to read, in truth, the *spirit* of the author . . . The voice of Seguin seemed to be like the voice of the forerunner crying in the wilderness, and my thoughts were filled with the immensity and importance of a work which should be able to reform the school and education. (MM, 42)

My own experience with Seguin's method inspired me with confidence in it. (D, 31) . . . For ten years I not only made practical experiments according to their methods, but through reverent meditation absorbed the works of these noble and consecrated men, who have left to humanity most vital proof of their obscure heroism. (MM, 46) . . . My intention was to keep in touch with the researches of others, but to make myself independent of them, proceeding to my work without preconceptions of any kind. (MM, 72)

. . . I attempted an original method for the teaching of reading and writing, a part of the education of the child which was most imperfectly treated in the works of both Itard and Seguin. (MM, 38) I succeeded in teaching a number of the idiots from the asylums both to read and to write so well that I was able to present them at a public school for an examination successfully . . . While everyone was admiring the progress of my idiots, I was searching for the reasons which could keep the happy healthy children of the common schools on so low a plane that they could be equalled in tests of intelligence by my unfortunate pupils.

I differed from my colleagues in that I instinctively felt that mental deficiency was more of an educational than a medical problem, (D, 22) . . . after I had left the school for deficients, and, little by little, I became convinced that similar methods applied to normal children would develop or set free their personality in a marvellous and surprising way. (MM, 33)

THE ADULT AND THE CHILD

One of Dr. Montessori's greatest concerns was the need for adults to change their thinking about the needs of the child; to first better ourselves, so that we could better teach the child by our example as well as by our words. The adult, in her opinion, was the greatest hindrance to the child's free and spontaneous development, and herein lies one of her most innovative insights, which opens up a whole new concept of early education. For her it was important to free the child from his role of dependency on adults if he was to develop into a truly free and independent person.

Direct intervention by the adult in the activity of the child will not help him. What he is able to do, he must do by himself, and it is important in these early years for the adult to do everything within his power to help the child do things on his own.

. . . children are human beings to whom respect is due, superior to us by reason of their "innocence" and of the greater possibilities of their future . . . Let us treat them . . . with all the kindness which we would wish to help to develop in them. (H, 133)

A child is a natural being living in the midst of adults. (S, 234) . . . A child must start from nothing and make his way into the company of adults . . . The adult is the child's creator, ruler, guardian, and benefactor. Never is anyone so utterly dependent upon another as a child is upon an adult. (S, 236) . . . The child must have a special function besides being merely smaller and weaker than the adult. (CE, 79) . . . if a child is to be treated differently than he is today, if he is to be saved from the conflicts that endanger his psychic life, a radical change, and one upon which everything else will depend, must first be made; and that change must be made in the adult. Indeed, since the adult claims that he is doing all that he can for his child and, as he further declares, he is already sacrificing himself out of love for him, he acknowledges that he is confronted with an unsurmountable problem. He must therefore have recourse to something that lies beyond his conscious and voluntary knowledge. (S, 18)

Adults have not understood children or adolescents and they are, as a consequence, in continual conflict with them . . . The adult must find within himself the still unknown error that prevents him from *seeing the child* as he is. (S, 19) . . . the adult looks upon himself as the child's creator and judges the child's actions as good or bad from the viewpoint of his own relations with the child. The adult makes himself the touchstone of what is good and evil in the child. He is infallible, the model upon which the child must be molded. Any deviation on the child's part from adult ways is regarded as an evil which the adult hastens to correct . . . An adult who acts in this way . . . unconsciously suppresses the development of the *child's own personality*. (S, 20) . . . if a child has within himself the key to his own personality, if he has a plan of development and laws to be observed, these must be delicate powers indeed, and an adult by his untimely interventions can prevent their secret realization.

However much we may love a child, from the first moment of its arrival among us we are instinctively on our gaurd against it. (S, 28) . . . This struggle between the love of the parents and the innocence of the child is carried on unconsciously. (S, 90) . . . We should remember that a child loves us and wants to obey. (S, 127) . . . an adult . . . substitutes himself in all the actions which the child would like to carry out by himself. He prevents the child from acting feely and thus makes himself the greatest obstacle to the child's natural development. (S, 110)

An adult who does not understand that a child needs to use his hands and does not recognize this as the first manifestation of an instinct for work can be an obstacle to the child's development. (S, 108) . . . If he is to develop his personality, it is necessary that the adult should hold himself in check and follow the lead given by the child. (S, 93)

. . . the child is not an inert being who owes everything he can do to us, as if he were an empty vessel that we have to fill. No, it is the child who makes the man, and no man exists who was not made by the child who he once was . . . it is the baby who produces the man . . . it is the child who absorbs material from the world about him; he who molds it into the man of the future. (AM, 15–16)

THE DISCOVERY OF THE CHILD

The Absorbent Mind

Montessori refers to the period of life between birth and three as the time when the intelligence and all the psychic faculties are being formed. Intelligence, according to her, is the ability to differentiate and to make judgments quickly and in an orderly manner. Man, unlike animals, is not born with preestablished behavior patterns, only with the ability to form them.

She spoke of the child's mind as the "absorbent mind" because of its great ability to learn and assimilate effortlessly and unconsciously from the world around him. While the child is absorbing from his environment, he is building into himself a part of his mental being. Through gradual and normal learning processes, behavior patterns are established and the powers of the adult mind are developed. She recognized that the young child in his formative stages absorbs almost all of his early learning from an environment in which he is placed: attitudes, language, movements, behavior. The environment of the classroom was prepared with this concept in mind.

There exists in the small child an unconscious mental state which is of a creative nature. We have called it the "Absorbent Mind." (CE, 85) . . . The child has an intelligence of this unconscious type, and that is what brings about his marvelous progress . . . The child *absorbs* these impressions not with his mind but with his life itself . . . Language provides the most obvious example. (AM, 24)

. . . The tiny child's *absorbent mind* finds all its nutriment in its surroundings . . . Especially at the beginning of life must we, therefore, make the environment as interesting and attractive as we can. (AM, 97) By absorbing what he finds about him, he forms his own personality . . . First, he takes in the world as a whole, then he analyzes it. (AM, 84–85) . . . The child creates his own "mental muscles," using for this what he finds in the world about him. We have named this type of mentality, *The Absorbent Mind*. . . . He constructs his mind step by step till it becomes possessed of memory, the power to understand, the ability to think . . . The discovery that the child has a mind able to absorb on its own account produces a revolution in education. We can now understand easily why the first period in human development, in which character is formed, is the most important. At no other age has the child greater need of an intelligent help, and any obstacle that impedes his creative work will lessen the chance he has of achieving perfection. (AM, 28) . . . He has a type of mind that goes beyond the concrete. He has the great power of imagination. (AM, 176)

Observations of the Child

Montessori throughout her life maintained that her most important contribution was the true "discovery of the child." Her medical background led her to the logical conclusion that to understand children better, much observation was necessary. Her knowledge of human development, based on these observations, formed the core to her method.

Her aim was to develop the *whole* personality of the child through motor, sensory, and intellectual activity. Theories were far less important to her than was the child himself. She had a love and respect for the child, and her concern for his welfare crossed the boundaries of race, religion, and creed.

When Dr. Montessori began working in the first Children's House, she kept intricate data on her observations of the children's mental and physical growth, development, habits and progress. She weighed the children every week, measured their height every month, and yearly took measurements of the circumference of their heads and chests, as well as advising a thorough yearly medical checkup by a physician. Nutrition and hygiene were integral parts of her program, with charts and records kept, and detailed procedures written out. It was the *whole* child that concerned Montessori, and his health and physical development paralleled the intellectual achievement.

Dr. Montessori drew up a list of the likes and dislikes of the children in the Casa dei Bambini to guide her in the application of her principles:

1. What he likes:
   Repetition of the exercise.
   Free choice.
   Control of error.
   Analysis of movements.
   Exercise of Silence.
   Good manners in social contacts.
   Order in environment.
   Care for personal cleanliness.
   Training of the senses.
   Writing separated from reading.

Writing before reading.
Reading without books.
Discipline in free activity.

2. What he rejects:
Rewards and punishments.
Spellers.
Lessons in common.
Programs and examinations
Toys and sweets.
A teacher's desk. (S, 169)

A colleague once said that Montessori looked at children much as a naturalist would look at bees, meaning it as the most flattering form of praise. In Montessori's own words.

. . . when dealing with children, there is greater need for observing than of probing. (S, 14) . . . a child possesses an active psychic life even when he cannot manifest it, and . . . must secrectly perfect this inner life over a long period of time. (S, 14) . . . It is the spirit of the child that can determine the course of human progress and lead it perhaps even to a higher form of civilization. (S, 9) . . . a child's spirit can be so deeply hidden that it is not immediately apparent . . . it is the child alone that can reveal the plan that is *natural* to man. (S, 23–24) . . . The child's way of doing things, has been for us an inexhaustible fountain of revelations. (AM, 177) . . . Studying these children and their mutual relationships in an atmosphere of freedom, the true secrets of society come to be revealed. (AM, 228)

Children decide on their actions under the prompting of natural laws . . . Inner forces affect his choice, and if somone usurps the function of this guide, the child is prevented from developing either his will or his concentration . . . a negative action is the interruption of work at fixed times in the daily program. (AM, 241) Growth comes from activity, not from intellectual understanding. Education, therefore, of little ones is important, especially from three to six years of age, because this is the embryonic period for the formation of character and of society, (just as the period from birth to three is that for forming the mind, and the prenatal period that for forming the body). What the child achieves between three and six does not depend on doctrine but on a divine directive which guides his spirit to construction. (AM, 242–243)

To find the interpretation of children's desires we must study them scientifically, for their desires are often unconscious, (H, 133) . . . we are here to offer to this life, which came into the world by itself, the *means* necessary for its development, and having done that we must await this development with respect. Let us leave the life *free* to develop within the limits of the good, and let us observe this inner life developing. (H, 134)

We discovered that education is not something which the teacher does, but that it is a natural process which develops spontaneously in the human being. It is not acquired by listening to words, but in virtue of experiences in which the child acts on his environment. (AM, 8) . . . It is true that we cannot make a genius. We can only give to each child the chance to fulfill his potential possibilities. (AM, 94) . . . we must offer the child the help he needs, and be at his service so that he does not have to walk alone . . . The child is truly a miraculous being, and this should be felt deeply by the educator. (AM, 121)

A child is an eager observer and is particularly attracted by the actions of adults and wants to imitate them. (S, 114) . . . before he can imitate, the child must first of all *understand* . . . The first efforts the child makes are not aimed at imitating, but *at forming in himself the capacity to imitate*; they are aimed at changing *himself* into the thing desired. (AM, 158–159) . . . There is—so to speak—in every child a painstaking teacher, so skilled that he obtains identical results in all children in all parts of the world. (AM, 6) . . . it is necessary that the *pupil perfect himself* through his own efforts . . . a man is not what he is because of the teachers he has had, but because of what he has done. (MM, 172) . . . children have a deep sense of personal dignity. (S, 154) . . . children construct their own characters, building up in themselves the qualities we admire. (AM, 208)

The child has to acquire physical independence by being self-sufficient; he must become of independent will by using in freedom his own power of choice; he must become capable of independent thought by working alone without interruption. The child's development follows a path of successive stages of independence, and our knowledge of this must guide us in our behavior towards him. We have to help the child to act, will and think for himself. This is the art of serving the spirit, an art which can be practiced to perfection only when working among children. (AM, 281) . . . The child is the spiritual building of mankind and obstacles to his free development are the stones in the wall by which the soul of man has become imprisoned. (AM, 221)

By the age of three, the child has already laid down the foundation of his personality as a human being, and only then does he need the help of special scholastic influences. (AM, 7) . . . Before three the functions are being created: after three they develop. (AM, 166) . . . The social rights of children must be recognized so that a world suited to their needs may be constructed for them. (S, 262)

The life of a child is not an abstraction; it is something that is lived by each one in particular. (D, 63) . . . Since a child is constantly growing, he is fascinated by everything that contributes to his development and becomes indifferent to idle occupations. (S, 149) . . . In order to develop his mind a child must have objects in his environment which he can hear and see . . . he must develop himself through his movements, through the work of his hands, he has need of objects with which he can work that provide motivation for his activity. (S, 101–102) Even sense objects . . . can have a powerful, suggestive influence upon a child, drawing out various activities like a magnet. (S, 114) . . . By nature man is an explorer and it is only by the discovery of the seemingly insignificant details that he advances. (S, 137) . . . we should really find the way to *teach* the child *how*, before *making him execute a task*. (MM, 261) . . . There is educational value in this idea of preparing oneself before trying, and of perfecting oneself before going on. To go forward without correcting his own mistakes, boldly attempting things which he does imperfectly, and of which he is as yet unworthy dulls the sensitiveness of the child's spirit toward his own errors. (MM, 292) . . . The greatest source of discouragement is the conviction that one is unable to do something. (S, 207) . . . Children feel a special interest for those things already rendered familiar to them (by absorption) in the earlier period. (AM, 172)

Growth and development depend upon a continued narrowing of the relationships between a child and his environment. (S, 227)

. . . To the casual onlooker the child seems to be learning exactitude and grace of action, to be refining his senses, to be learning how to read and write, how to be a man of prompt and resolute will. (MM, 365) . . . Within the child lies the fate of the future. (S, 255) . . . We serve the future by protecting the present. (AM, 195) . . . It is solely from a child that man is formed. (S, 236)

The Child and Work

Work and play are often the same thing to the young child. The children Montessori observed at the Children's House showed great interest, enthusiasm, and actual plesaure in their work, and the work itself provided stimulus for a sense of achievement. The children were allowed to work at their own rate of speed, completing the "cycles of activity" so necessary to their growth and development.

A child's instinct for work is a proof that work is instinctive to man and characteristic of the species. (S, 228) . . . His objective in working is the work itself, and when he has repeated an exercise and brought his own activities to an end, this end is independent of external factors. (S, 240)

Once the habit of work is formed, we must supervise it with a scrupulous accuracy, graduating the exercises as experience has taught us . . . The phenomenon of discipline needs as preparation a series of complete actions, such as are presupposed in the genuine application of really educative method . . . The end is obtained not by attacking the mistake and fighting it, but by developing activity in spontaneous work. (MM, 350) . . . To have learned something is for the child only a point of departure. When he has learned the meaning of an exercise, then he begins to enjoy repeating it, and he does repeat it an infinite number of times, with the most evident satisfaction. He enjoys executing that act because by means of it he is developing his psychic activities. (MM, 357) . . . Each one of them perfects himself through his own powers, and goes forward guided by that inner force which distinguishes him as an individual. (MM, 373)

The children work by themselves, and, in doing so make a conquest of active discipline, and independence in all the acts of daily life, just as through daily conquests they progress in intellectual development. (MM, 374) . . . The process of living is, for the child, an extension and amplification of himself; the older he gets, the stronger and more intelligent he becomes. His work and activity help him to acquire this strength and intelligence . . . there is no competition in childhood, because no one can do for the child the work he has to do to build the man he is making. No one, in short, can do his growing for him. (AM, 30) . . . A child develops through personal effort and engagement. (S. 117)

THE SENSITIVE PERIODS

According to Montessori, people form all aspects of their personalities through their own experiences in interacting with their environment. Throughout life, people possess a sensitivity to and eagerness for assimilation. These "sensitive periods" are most readily apparent in the early years of childhood and involve the period in which the child is particularly receptive to certain stimuli. A particular sensitivity toward something lasts only until a necessary need is fulfilled. If parents are aware of these periods, much can be done to help the child utilize them in understanding and mastering his environment at the peak of his particular sensitive period. The flexibility of the method and its intent that each child be allowed to progress at his own rate of speed makes these sensitive periods *optimal*.

Birth–3 years	Absorbent mind
	Sensory experiences
1½–3 years	Language development
1½–4 years	Coordination and muscle development
	Interest in small objects
2–4 years	Refinement of movement
	Concern with truth and reality
	Awareness of order sequence in time and space
2½–6 years	Sensory refinement
3–6 years	Susceptibility to adult influence
3½–4½ years	Writing
4–4½ years	Tactile sense
4½–5½ years	Reading

A sensitive period refers to a special sensibility which a creature acquires in its infantile state . . . It is a transient disposition and limited to the acquisition of a particular trait. Once this trait, or characteristic, has been acquired, the special sensibility disappears . . . A child learns to adjust himself and make acquisitions in his sensitive periods . . . It is this sensibility which enables a child to come into contact with the external world in a particularly intense manner . . . When one of these psychic passions is exhausted, another is enkindled. Childhood thus passes from conquest to conquest in a constant rhythm that constitutes its joy and happiness . . . When the sensitive period has disappeared, intellectual victories are reported through reasoning processes, voluntary efforts and the toil of research. And from the torpor of indifference is born the weariness of labor. (S, 46–49)

A child's different inner sensibilities enable him to choose from his complex environment what is suitable and necessary for his growth. They make the child sensitive to some things, but leave him indifferent to others. When a particular sensitiveness is aroused in a child, it is like a light that shines on some objects but not on others, making them his whole world. (S, 51)

A child has a sensitive period which lasts until he is almost five years old, and which enables him to assimilate images from his environment in a truly prodigious fashion. He is an observer actively receiving these images through his senses. (S, 76)

It is necessary to offer those exercises which correspond to the need of development felt by an organism, and if the child's age has carried him past a certain need, it is never possible to obtain in its fullness, a development which missed its proper moment. (MM, 358)

INDEPENDENCE

For Montessori the acquisition of independence, the nature of [which] changes at each of the child's different stages of development, was a most important part of the educational process and necessary to the child's normal development. All children possess a need and determination to strive for independence; to be able to do for themselves what others have previously done for them. It is an essential part of "growing up" and the ultimate goal of the method, which is a sequential progression of steps leading to self-mastery and functional independence.

No one can be free unless he is independent . . . In reality, *he who is served is limited* in his independence . . . Any pedagogical action, if it is to be efficacious in training of little children, must tend to *help* the children to advance upon this road of independence . . . We habitually *serve* children; and this is not only an act of servility toward them, but it is dangerous, since it tends to suffocate their useful, spontaneous activity . . . We do not stop to think that the child *who does not do, does not know how to do* . . . Who does not know that to *teach* a child to feed himself, to wash and dress himself, is a much more tedious and difficult work, calling for infinitely greater patience than feeding, washing and dressing the child one's self? (MM, 97–98)

. . . The child's nature is to aim directly and energetically at functional independence. Development takes the form of a drive toward an ever greater independence . . . The child's conquest of independence are the basic steps in what is called his "natural development" . . . it can be defined as the gaining of successive levels of independence. (AM, 83)

Learning to speak . . . and the power it brings of intelligent converse with others, is a most impressive further step along the path of independence . . . at one year of age, the child begins to walk, and this sets him free from yet another prison . . . So man develops by stages, and the freedom he enjoys comes from these steps towards independence taken in turn . . . his independence is a physiological state, a change wrought by the process of growth. Truly it is a nature which affords the child the opportunity to grow; it is nature which bestows independence upon him and guides him to success in achieving his freedom. (AM, 85)

The child's first instinct is to carry out his actions by himself, without anyone helping him, and his first conscious bid for independence is made when he defends himself against those who try to do the action for him. To succeed by himself he intensifies his efforts. (AM, 91)

Happiness is not the whole aim of education. A man must be independent in his powers and character, able to work and assert his mastery over all that depends on him. *This was the light in which childhood revealed itself to us, once consciousness had come to birth and begun to take control*. (AM, 170)

We must make of the future generations, *powerful men*, and by that we mean men who are independent and free. (MM, 101)

OBEDIENCE

Obedience is an essential component of the Montessori classroom, and it is this advanced form of behavior from such young children that most astounds the visitor. It is necessary to understand how obedience develops in the young child in order to help him achieve his *ultimate goal of becoming normalized*. It is a characteristic that must be learned gradually as the intellect and reasoning powers develop. All children possess an innate desire to please.

Obedience appears in the child as a latent instinct as soon as his personality begins to take form. (MM, 367) . . . Before the child is three he cannot obey unless the order he receives corresponds with one of his vital urges. (AM, 258)

There is nothing more harmful than discouragement just when new formations are being made. If the child is not yet master of his actions, if he cannot obey even his own will, so much the less can he obey the will of someone else . . . Discipline is made to rest on threats and fear, so we end by concluding that the disobedient child is wicked and the obedient one good . . . The basic error is to suppose that a person's will must necessarily be broken before it can obey, meaning before it can accept and follow another person's directions . . . Will and obedience then go hand in hand, inasmuch as the will is a prior foundation in the order of development, and obedience is a later stage resting on this foundation . . . Obedience is seen as something which develops in the child in much the same way as other aspects of his character. (AM, 256–259)

. . . inner discipline is something to come, and not something already present . . . The first level of obedience is that in which the child can obey, but not always . . . The second level is when the child can always obey, or rather when there are no longer any obstacles deriving from his lack of control . . . the third level . . . is turned toward a personality whose superiority he feels . . . The child can absorb another person's wishes and express them in his own behavior. And this is the highest form of obedience to which present day education ever aspires. The ordinary teacher asks only that she be obeyed . . . The power to obey is the last phase in the development of the will, which in its turn has made obedience possible. (AM, 260)

If discipline is to be lasting, its foundations must be laid in this way and these first days are the most difficult for the directness . . . I do not know what happened in the soul of these children whom we found it necessary to discipline, but certainly the conversion was always complete and lasting. They showed great pride in learning how to work and how to conduct themselves, and always showed a very tender affection for the teacher and for me. (MM, 93)

LIBERTY, FREEDOM, AND ORDER

Freedom and structure are considered to be the two fundamental poles of Montessori education, and yet which comes first becomes a case similar to "which came first, the chicken or the egg?" There are those who feel that freedom makes sense only if there is structure and self-discipline. Is freedom gained by a child by realizing the limits of what he can do, or is it necessary to experience freedom and encounter his impulses prior to participating in setting limits and imposing structures and controls? Either way, there is a definite interplay between the two—freedom and structure—in every Montessori classroom. The freedom and liberty of the child in a Montessori classroom come about through the development of order within the child.

The pedagogical method of *observation* has for its base the *liberty* of the child; and *liberty* is *activity*. Discipline must come through liberty . . . We call an individual disciplined when he is master of himself, and can, therefore, regulate his own conduct when it shall be necessary to follow some rule of life . . . Since the child now learns to *move* rather than to *sit still*, he prepares himself not for the school, but for life . . . The liberty of the child should have as its *limit* the collective interest; as its *form* what we universally consider good breeding. (MM, 86–87)

Real freedom is a consequence of development; it is the development of latent guides, aided by education. Development is active. It is the construction of the personality, reached by effort and one's own experiences; it is the long road which every child must travel to attain maturity . . . Development cannot be taught . . . we leave the children *free* in their work, and in all actions which are not of a disturbing kind. That is, we eliminate disorder, which is "bad," but allow that which is orderly and "good" the most complete liberty of manifestation . . . The child . . . through this natural tendency is let to coordinate his movements and to collect impressions, especially sensations of the touch, so that when prevented he rebels, and this rebellion forms almost the whole of his "naughtiness." (H, 183)

Freedom without organization of work would be useless. The child left *free* without means of work would go to waste . . . The organization *of the work*, therefore, is the corner-stone of this new structure of goodness; but even that organization would be in vain without the *liberty* to make use of it, and without freedom for the expansion of all those energies which spring from the satisfaction of the child's highest activities . . . we have made a contribution to the cause of goodness by removing obstacles which were the cause of violence and rebellion. (H, 188–189) . . . An educational method that shall have *liberty* as its basis must intervene to help the child to a conquest of these various obstacles. (MM, 95)

. . . nature endows a child with a sensitiveness to order. . . . a child has a twofold sense of order. One of these is external and pertains to his perception of his relations with his environment. The second is internal and makes him aware of the different parts of his own body and their relative positions. (S, 68–69)

A very important and mysterious period is the one which makes a child extremely sensitive to order. This sensitiveness appears in a child's first year and continues on through the second . . . Order consists in recognizing the place for each object in relation to its environment and in remembering where each thing should be. (S, 61) . . . when order is established everything advances smoothly. (S, 19)

MOVEMENT AND ACTIVITY

Movement and activity are natural functions of childhood, and learning comes through them. Everything in the Montessori school environment is arranged to this end, with a wide assortment of materials and the freedom to move about. Activity becomes increasingly important to development, and the young child needs many opportunities for observation, movement and exploration. It is movement that starts the intellectual working. Manipulative exercises involving the use of the hand and mind together make the child an active participant in his own learning process.

A child is a discoverer. He is an amorphous, splendid being in search of his own proper form . . . The importance of physical activity or movement in physic development should be emphasized. (S, 117–121) . . . Everything in the living world is active. Life is activity at its peak, and it is only through activity that the perfectionments of life can be sought and gained. (AM, 91)

A child gains experience through exercises and movement. He coordinates his own movements and records the emotions he experiences in coming into contact with the external world. (S, 237) . . . Movement is another of the child's great acquisitions . . . The movements the child acquires are not chosen haphazardly but are fixed, in the sense that each proceeds out of a particular period of development. When the child begins to move, his mind, being able to absorb, has already taken in his surroundings . . . He is directed by a mysterious power, great and wonderful, that he incarnates little by little. In this way, he becomes a man. He does it with his hands, by experience, first in play and then through work. The hands are the instruments of man's intelligence . . . He constructs his mind step by step till it becomes possessed of memory, the power to understand, the ability to think. (AM, 27)

A child who is free to act not only seeks to gather sensible impressions from his environment but he also shows a love for exactitude in the carrying out of his actions. (S, 121) . . . Activity freely chosen becomes their regular way of living. The healing of their disorders is the doorway to this kind of life. (AM, 207)

. . . the first thing that strikes us is a phenomenon of concentration on some one thing . . . after concentration will come perseverance . . . The first essential for the child's development is concentration. It lays the whole basis for his character and social behavior . . . The child who concentrates is immensely happy . . . (AM, 216 & 272)

. . . the child's mind can acquire culture at a much earlier age than is generally supposed, but his way of taking in knowledge is by certain kinds of activity which involve movement. (AM, 172) . . . the human hand . . . allows the mind to reveal itself . . . it enables the whole being to enter into special relationships with its environment . . . His hands under the guidance of his intellect transform this environment and thus enable him to fulfill his mission in the world. (S, 100) . . . The hands . . . are connected with mental life . . . the child's intelligence can develop to a certain level without the help of his hand. But if it develops with his hand, then the level it reaches is higher, and the child's character is stronger. (AM, 152)

The education of the movements is very complex, as it must correspond to all the coordinated movements which the child has to establish in his physiological organism. The child, if left without guidance, is disorderly in his movements, and these disorderly movements are the *special characteristic of the little child* . . . in these movements the little one is seeking the very exercise which will organize and coordinate the movements useful to man . . . Once a direction is given to them, the child's movements are made towards a definite end, so that he himself grows quiet and contented, and becomes an active worker, a being calm and full of joy. This education of movements is one of the principal factors in producing that outward appearance of "discipline" to be found in the "Children's Houses." (H, 52–53)

THE METHOD

There was no method to be seen, what was seen was the child . . . The first thing to be done, therefore, is to discover the true nature of a child and then assist him in his normal development. (S, 166–167)

My method is scientific, both in its substance and in its aims. (H, 36) . . . the importance of my method does not lie in the organization itself, but in the *effects which it produces on the child*. It is the *child* who proves the value of this method by his spontaneous manifestations, which seem to reveal the laws of man's inner development. (H, 182)

Our aim in education in general is twofold, biological and social. From the biological side we wish to help the natural development of the individual, from the social standpoint it is our aim to prepare the individual for the environment . . . All education of little children must be governed by this principle—to help the natural *psychic and physical development of the child*. (MM, 216)

. . . the special circumstances surrounding the children were a suitable environment, a humble teacher, and material objects adapted to their needs. (S, 168) . . . The method used by me is that of making a pedagogical experiment with a didactic object and awaiting the spontaneous reaction of the child. (MM, 167) . . . the children were given special material with which to work. They were attracted by these objects which perfected their sense perceptions, enabling them to analyze and facilitate their movements. These materials also taught them how to concentrate in a way that no vocal instruction ever could have done. (S, 168)

Our educational aim with very young children must be to *aid the spontaneous development of the mental, spiritual and physical personality,* and not to make of the child a cultured individual in the commonly accepted sense of the term . . . after we have offered to the child such didactic material as we adapted to provoke the development of his senses, we must wait until the activity known as observation develops. And herein lies *the art of the educator;* in knowing how to measure the action by which we help the young child's personality to develop. (MM, 230–231)

Surrounded by interesting things to do, they could repeat the exercises at will, and went from one spell of concentration to another. Once the children had reached this stage, and could work and focus their minds on something of real interest to them, their defects disappeared. The disorderly became orderly, the passive became active, and the troublesome disturbing child became a help in the classroom. This result made us understand that their former defects had been acquired and were not innate . . . all these disturbances came from a single cause, which was insufficient nourishment for the life of the mind . . . What advice can we give to mothers? Their children need to work at an interesting occupation: they should not be helped unnecessarily, nor interrupted, once they have begun to do something intelligent. Sweetness, severity, medicine, do not help if the child is mentally hungry . . . Man is an intelligent being, and needs mental food almost more than physical food. Unlike the animals, he has to build up his own behavior. If the child is placed upon a path in which he can organize his conduct and construct his mental life, all will be well . . . His health is restored because his mind is normalized. (AM, 199–200)

They could now choose their own occupations according to their own particular preferences . . . The principle *of free choice* was thus added to that of *repetition of the exercise* . . . I then came to realize that everything about a child should not only be in order, but that it should be *proportioned to the child's use*, and that interest and concentration arise specifically from the elimination of what is confusing and superfluous, (S, 148) . . . the majority of our children become calm as they go through such exercises, because their nervous system is at rest. (MM, 362)

The technique of my method as it follows the guidance of the natural physiological and psychical development of the child, may be divided into three parts: Motor education, Sensory education, Language. (H, 50) . . . The functions to be established by the child fall into two groups: 1) the motor functions by which he is to secure his balance and learn to walk, and to coordinate his movements; 2) the sensory functions through which, receiving sensations from his environment, he lays the foundations of his intelligence by a continual exercise of observation, comparison and judgment. In this way he gradually comes to be acquainted with his environment and to develop his intelligence. (H, 34–35)

Both the ages of the children, and the deep interests they show, have given us much noteworthy material; the more so as their actions have so much in common with the highest characteristics of mankind . . . one can see a process of construction going on. (AM, 216) . . . The greatest triumph of our educational method should always be this: *to bring about the spontaneous progress of the child*. (MM, 228)

I believe that I have by my method established the conditions necessary to the development of scientific pedagogy . . . It is my hope that, *starting from the individual study of the child* educated with our method, other educators will set forth the results of their experiments. These are the pedagogical books which await us in the future. (MM, 370–373)

THE PREPARED ENVIRONMENT

With the realization that children absorb unconsciously from their environment, it became necessary to provide a seemingly perfect learning environment for developing children. This structured environment for learning involves use of a wide range of *didactic apparatus*, varied activities reflecting all aspects of the child's development, with everything being aesthetically pleasing and geared to the child's size, needs, and interests.

Montessori felt that self-motivation was the key to sound learning. To her the child came first, the curriculum second. Through her observations she found that these children thrived on learning and that they chose those materials which seemed to fulfill a specific need within them. The focus of the Montessori curriculum is on mastery of one's self and environment. The wide array of materials has been designed to serve this purpose and to help each individual develop and perfect his own capabilities. The prepared environment is meant to provide exposure to materials and experiences to aid the child in developing intellectual, physical, and psychological abilities. These materials are only symbols, acting as aids, to the child's self-construction.

The environment and the materials have controls built into them to eliminate obstacles, to encourage beneficial activities, and to correct the child's errors. The spontaneous use of these auto-instructional materials enables the child to focus his attention upon the mastery of subjects and skills. Each child should be given the opportunity to work freely in self-chosen tasks commensurate with his needs.

Repetition is necessary for the child to refine his senses, perfect his skills and build up competency and knowledge. In order to repeat, the child must understand the idea or concept that is to be repeated. Repetition is a necessary step in self-development and the child revels in repeating those things which he knows best and does well.

The child who undertakes something for the first time is extremely slow and persevering. He patiently overcomes the difficulties presented in an attempt to accomplish his goal. He must be left free to repeat things in order to learn and fulfill his need to accumulate experiences. He needs to complete what Dr. Montessori called his "cycles of activity"—those periods of concentration on a particular task that should be worked to completion. Not to allow this causes the developing child great frustration. It is the inner need that compels him to work so long and hard at a particular tsak, long after the older child or adult would have lost interest and grown weary.

There is a great sense of community within the Montessori classroom, where children of differing ages work together in an atmosphere of cooperation rather than competitiveness. There is respect for the environment and for the individuals within it, which comes through experience of freedom within the community.

What is most characteristic of our system of education is the emphasis that is placed upon the environment . . . To assist a child we must provide him with an environment which will enable him to develop freely. A child is passing through a period of self-realization, and it is enough simply to open up the door for him . . . In an open environment, that is, one that is suitable to his age, a child's psychic life should develop naturally and reveal its inner secrets. (S, 134–135)

It is through the environment that the individual is molded and brought to perfection . . . since a child is formed by his environment he has need of precise and determined guides and not simply some vague constructive formulae. (S, 43 & 66)

Sometimes very small children in a proper environment develop a skill and exactness in their work that can only surprise us . . . An adult environment is not a suitable environment for children. (S, 107 & 133) . . . there must be a suitable environment for the child's growth. Obstacles must be reduced to a minimum and the surroundings should provide the necessary means for the exercise of those activities which develop a child's energies . . . adults should not be an obstacle to a child's independent activities, nor should they carry out for him those activities by means of which a child reaches maturity. (S, 135) . . . *The environment* acts more strongly upon the individual life the less fixed and strong this individual life may be. (MM, 106)

The Children's House

The Children's House is the *environment* which is offered to the child that he may be given the opportunity of developing his activities . . . The central and principal room of the building, is the room for "intellectual work" . . . The special characteristic of the equipment of these houses is that it is adapted for children and not adults. They contain not only didactic material specially fitted for the intellectual development of the child, but also a complete equipment for the management of the miniature family. (H, 37–38)

The Children's House has a twofold importance: the social importance which it assumes through its peculiarity of being a school within the house, and its purely pedagogic importance gained through its methods for the education of very young children, of which I now made a trial. (MM, 44)

The principal modification in the matter of school furnishings is the abolition of desks, and benches or stationary chairs. I have had tables made with wide, solid, octagonal legs, spreading in such a way that the tables are at the same time solidly firm and very light, so light, indeed, that two four-year-old children can easily carry them about. These tables are rectangular and sufficiently large to accommodate two children on the long side, there being room for three if they sit rather close together. There are smaller tables at which one child may work alone. I also designed and had manufactured little chairs . . . These are very light and of an attractive shape . . . a little washstand, so low that it can be used by even a three-year-old child . . . a series of long low cupboards, especially designed for the reception of the didactic materials . . . Our little tables and our various types of chairs are all light and easily transported, and we permit the child to *select* the position which he finds most comfortable. He can *make himself comfortable* as well as seat himself in his own place. And this freedom is not only an external sign of the liberty, but a means of education. (MM, 81–84)

In our schools we give everything needed so that the child can imitate the actions he sees in his home, or in the country in which he lives. But we have implements specially made for him, of the right size to suit his diminutive proportions and strength. The room is dedicated to him, and he is free to move about in it, talk·

and apply himself to intelligent and formative kinds of work (AM, 169)

We started by equipping the child's environment with a little of everything, and left the children to choose those things they preferred . . . A child chooses what helps him to construct himself . . . There is only one specimen of each object, and if a piece is in use when another child wants it, the latter—if he is normalized— will wait for it to be released. Important social qualities derive from this. The child comes to see that he must respect the work of others, not because someone has said that he must, but because this is a reality that he meets in his daily experience . . . waiting one's turn, becomes an habitual part of life which always grows more mature. (AM, 223–224)

The charm of social life is in the number of different types that one meets . . . What matters is to mix the ages . . . we have with our methods the advantage of being able to teach in one room, children of very different ages . . . Each one of them perfects himself through his own powers, and goes forward guided by that inner force which distinguishes him as an individual. (MM, 373) . . . Our schools show that children of different ages help one another. The younger ones see what the older ones are doing, and ask for explanations . . . There are many things which no teacher can convey to a child of three, but a child of five can do it with the utmost ease. (AM, 226)

Our dividing walls are only waist-high partitions, and there is always access from one classroom to the next. Children are free to pass to and from between classrooms. (AM, 227)

The child's progress does not depend only on his age, but also on being free to look about him. Our schools are alive . . . There is among children an evident sense of community . . . Just as the older ones are drawn to the younger, and vice versa, so are the normalized drawn to the newcomers, and these to those already acclimatized . . . A society like this seems to be more united by the *absorbent mind* than it does by the conscious mind. (AM, 228–232)

Men do not form a society just by having individual aims and undertaking each his own work, as the children do in our schools. The final form of human society is based on organization. (AM, 236) . . . The children in our schools are free, but that doesn't mean there is no organization. Organization, in fact, is necessary, and if the children are to be free to *work*, it must be even more thorough than in the ordinary schools . . . if a child has to be rewarded or punished, it means he lacks the capacity to guide himself. (AM, 224–245)

. . . the children must be free to choose their own occupations, just as they must never be interrupted in their spontaneous activity . . . Free choice is one of the highest of all the mental processes. (AM, 263 & 271) . . . Choice and execution are the prerogatives and conquests of a liberated soul . . . The school must give the child's spirit space and opportunity for expansion. (AM, 274 & 264)

. . . there are objects which permit the child who uses them to attain a determined goal. There are, for example, simple frames which enable a child to learn how to button, lace, hook, or tie things together. There are also washbasins where a child can wash his hands, brooms with which he can sweep the floor, dusters so that he can clean the furniture, brushes for shining his shoes or cleaning his clothes. All these objects invite a child to do something, to carry out a real task with a practical goal to be obtained. To spread out carpets and roll them up after they have been used, to spread a tablecloth for dinner and to fold it up and replace it carefully after the meal is finished, to set the table completely, to eat correctly and afterwards to remove the dishes and wash them, placing each object in its proper place in the cupboard, are tasks which not only require increasing skills but also a gradual development of character because of the patience necessary for their execution and the sense of responsibility for their successful accomplishment . . . these activities are called "exercises in practical life" because the children lead a practical life and do ordinary housework with a devotion and accuracy that becomes remarkably calm and dignified.

Beside the various objects which the children are taught to use for their "practical life," there are many others which lend themselves to the gradual development and refinement of a child's intellect. These are, for example, various materials for the education of the senses, for learning the alphabet, numbers, and reading, writing, and arithmetic. These objects are called "materials for development" to distinguish them from those used in practical life.

When we speak of "environment" we include the sum total of objects which a child can freely choose and use as he pleases . . . according to his needs and tendencies. (D, 64–65)

The Teacher

The Montessori teacher acts as the keeper of this prepared environment; she is not the focal point in the classroom. This is a distinction shared by her and the children, with the teacher serving as a link between the children and the prepared environment. Though Montessori tried to deemphasize the role of the teacher, she still remains an important factor in the classroom, and her influence, however subtle, is strongly felt.

In speaking of the role of the teacher, Montessori closed her address to an audience in India with these words, which she called a reminder and syllabus to her teachers:

Help us, O God, to enter into the secret of childhood, so that we may know, love and serve the child in accordance with the laws of thy justice and following thy holy will.(AM, 286)

The first thing required of a teacher is that he be rightly disposed for his task . . . It is not sufficient to have a merely theoretical knowledge of education. (S, 182) . . . The first step an intending Montessori teacher must take is to prepare herself . . . The teacher, when she begins to work in our schools, must have a kind of faith that *the child will reveal himself* through work. (AM, 276) . . . We insist on the fact that a teacher must prepare himself interiorly by systematically studying himself so that he can tear out his most deeply rooted defects, those in fact which impede his relations with children . . . First remove the beam from your own eye and then you will see clearly how to remove the speck from the eye of the child. (S, 182)

To prepare teachers in the method of the experimental sciences is not an easy matter . . . It is my belief that the thing which we should cultivate in our teachers is more the *spirit* than the mechanical skill of the scientist; that is, the *direction* of the *preparation* should be toward the spirit rather than toward the mechanism. (MM, 7 & 9) . . . From the child itself he will learn how to perfect himself as an educator . . . we must know how to call to the *man* which lies dormant within the soul of the child. (MM, 13 & 37) . . . We teachers can only help the work going on, as servants wait upon a master (AM, 9)

. . . the teacher must bring not only the capacity, but the desire, to observe natural phenomena . . . she must become a passive, much more than an active, influence, and her passivity shall be composed of anxious scientific curiosity, and of absolute *respect* for the phenomenon which she wishes to observe . . . We cannot know the consequences of suffocating a *spontaneous action* at the time when the child is just beginning to be active; perhaps we suffocate life itself. (MM, 87) . . . The teacher must be quiet and passive, waiting patiently and almost withdrawing herself from the scene, so as to efface her own personality and thus allow plenty of room for the child's spirit to expand . . . If the teacher cannot recognize the difference between pure impulse, and the spontaneous energies which spring to life in a tranquilized spirit, then her action will bear no fruit . . . Only when the teacher has learned to discriminate can she become an observer and guide. (AM, 264–265) . . . the teacher . . . by his passive attitude removes from the children the obstacle that is created by his own activity and authority. (S, 135)

. . . the teacher must not limit her action to *observation*, but must proceed to *experiment* . . . In this method the lesson corresponds to an *experiment* . . . The lessons . . . are individual, and brevity must be one of their chief characteristics . . . Another quality is its *simplicity* . . . The third quality of the lesson is its *objectivity*. The lesson must be presented in such a way that the personality of the teacher shall disappear. There shall remain in evidence only the *object* to which she wishes to call the attention of the child. (AM, 108) . . . The teacher shall observe whether the child interests himself in the object, how he is interested in it, for how long, etc., even noticing the expressions of his face. And she must take great care not to offend the principles of liberty. (MM, 107–109) . . . *The essential thing is for the task to arouse such an interest that it engages the child's whole personality.* (AM, 206)

The teacher's mission always has for its aim something constant and exact . . . She bears in mind the words . . . "He must grow while I diminish. (AM, 274) . . . It is necessary for the teacher to guide the child without letting him feel her presence too much, so that she may be always ready to supply the desired help, but may never be the obstacle between the child and his experience. (H, 130) . . . To stimulate life,—leaving it then free to develop, to unfold—herein lies the first task of the educator . . . When the teacher shall have touched, in this way, soul for soul, each one of her pupils, awakening and inspiring the life within them as if she were an invisible spirit, she will then possess each soul, and a sign, a single word from her shall suffice; for each one will feel her in a living and vital way, will recognize her and will listen to her. (MM, 115–116)

. . . the teacher teaches *little* and observes *much*, . . . For this reason I have changed the name of teacher into that of directress . . . The directress . . . must have a clear idea of the two factors which enter into her works; the guidance of the child, and the individual exercises. (MM, 173–173) . . . The directress must intervene to lead the child from sensations to ideas—from the concrete to the abstract, and to the association of ideas . . . when she gives a lesson she must seek to limit the field of the child's consciousness to the object of the lesson, as, for example, during the sense education she isolated the sense which she wished the child to exercise. (MM, 224)

The teacher, by doing the exercise herself, first shows the child how the pieces of each set should be arranged, but it will often happen that the child learns, not directly from her, but by watching his companions . . . it is the *repetition of the exercise* which, by refining his powers of observation, will lead him sooner or later to *correct himself*. (H, 76)

. . . the teacher must be warned of two things: the first, not to *insist* by repeating the lesson; and second, *not to make the child feel that he has made a mistake*, or that he is not understood. (MM, 109)

However desirable it may be to furnish a sense education as a basis for intellectual ideas, it is nevertheless advisable at the same time to associate the *language* with these *perceptions*. In this connection I have found excellent for use with normal children, *the three periods* of which the lesson according to Seguin consists:

First period. The association of the sensory perception with the name. For example, we present to the child, two colours, red and blue. Presenting the red, we say simply, "This is the red," and presenting the blue, "This is the blue." Then we lay the spools upon the table under the eyes of the child.
Second period. Recognition of the object corresponding to the name. We say to the child, "Give me the red," and then, "Give me the blue."
Third period. The remembering of the name corresponding to the object. We ask the child, showing him the object, "What is this?" and he should respond, "Red." (MM, 177–178)

The teacher becomes the keeper and custodian of the environment . . . The essential charm of a house is its cleanliness and order, with everything in its place, dusted, bright and cheerful. She makes this her first consideration. The teacher in the school must not do otherwise. All the apparatus is to be kept meticulously in order, beautiful and shining, in perfect condition. Nothing may be missing, so that to the child it always seems new, complete and ready for use. This means that the teacher also must be attractive, pleasing in appearance, tidy and clean, calm and dignified . . . The teacher's appearance is the first step to gaining the child's confidence and respect . . . Every action of the teacher's can become a call and an invitation to the children. (AM, 277–278)

Finally, the time comes in which the children begin to take an interest in something; usually, in the exercises of practical life, for experience shows that it is useless and harmful to give the children sensorial and cultural apparatus before they are ready to benefit from it. Before introducing this kind of material, one must wait till the children have acquired the power to concentrate on something . . . When the child begins to show interest . . . the teacher must *not interrupt*, because this interest corresponds with natural laws and opens up a whole cycle of new activities . . . The great prnciple which brings success to the teacher is this: as soon as concentration has begun, act as if the child does not exist. (AM, 270–280)

To serve the children is to feel one is serving the spirit of man, a spirit which has to free itself . . . At first the teacher will say, "I have seen the child as he ought to be, and found him better than I could have ever supposed" . . . What is the greatest sign of success for a teacher thus transformed? It is to be able to say, "The children are now working as if I did not exist." (AM, 282–283)

The Materials and the Lessons

. . . it is well to cultivate a friendly feeling towards error, to treat it as a companion inseparable from our lives, as something having a purpose, which it truly has . . . If we seek perfection, we must pay attention to our own defects, for it is only by correcting these that we can improve ourselves . . . mistakes, to us, have a particular importance, and to correct or eliminate them, we have first of all to know them . . . We call it "control of error." (AM, 246–247) . . . any kind of indicator which tells us whether we are going toward our goal, or away from it . . . Our apparatus is always designed to have this property of offering visible and tangible checks . . . unless I can correct myself, I shall have to seek the help of someone else, who may not know any better than I do. How much better it is if I can recognize my own mistakes, and then correct them! . . . Errors divide men, but their correction is a means of union. (AM, 248–50)

. . . the control of the error is in *the material itself*, and the child has concrete evidence of it. The desire of the child to attain an end which he knows, leads him to correct himself. It is not a teacher who makes him notice his mistake and shows him how to correct it, but it is a complex work of the child's own intelligence which leads to such a result . . . The aim is an inner one, namely, that the child train himself to observe; that he be led to make comparisons between objects, to form judgements, to reason and to decide; and it is in the indefinite repetition of this exercise of attention and of intelligence that a real development ensues. (H, 71)

The didactic material *controls every error*. The child proceeds to correct himself, doing this in various ways . . . it is precisley in these errors that the educational importance of the didactic material lies . . . This self-correction leads the child to concentrate his attention upon the differences of dimensions, and to compare the various pieces. (MM, 171)

The didactic material, in fact, does not offer to the child the "content" of the mind, but the *order* for that "content." It causes him to distinguish identities from differences, extreme differences from fine gradations, and to classify, under conceptions of quality and of quantity, the most varying sensations appertaining to surfaces, colors, dimension, forms and sounds. The mind has formed itself by a special exercise of attention, observing, comparing and classifying. The mental attitude acquired by such an exercise leads the child to make ordered observations in his environment, observations which prove as interesting to him as discoveries, and so stimulate him to multiply them indefinitely and to form in his mind a rich "content" of "clear ideas." (H, 137)

Our didactic material renders auto-education possible, permits a methodical education of the senses. Not upon the ability of the teacher does such education rest, but upon the didactic system. This represents objects which, first, attract the spontaneous attention of the child, and second, contain a rational gradation of stimuli. (MM, 175) . . . My didactic material offers to the child the *means* for what may be called "sensory education" (H, 65) . . . When the child educates himself, and when the control and correction of errors is yielded to the didactic materials, there *remains for the teacher nothing but to observe.* (MM, 173)

PRACTICAL APPLICATIONS OF THE THEORY

Sensory Education

Montessori agreed with Aristotle's philosophy that there was nothing in the intellect which does not first exist in the senses.

Through systematically working in successive steps with the sensory apparatus, and developing and refining the five senses, the child builds a solid foundation for his intellectual activity. The lessons were designed to enable the child to sort out and digest the large number of impressions he possesses, to assimilate additional ones through experience, and to stimulate and refine the child's powers of observation preliminary to acquiring judgment and understanding.

The hands and mind work together, making the learning

experience one of doing rather than of simply observing. The child becomes an active participant, enthusiastically absorbing knowledge and developing perception and manual dexterity.

The first of the child's organs to begin functioning are his senses. (AM, 84) . . . It is necessary to begin the education of the senses in the formative period, if we wish to perfect this sense development with the education which is to follow. The education of the senses would be begun methodically in infancy, and should continue during the entire period of instruction which is to prepare the individual for life in society. (MM, 221)

. . . the period of life between the ages of thee and seven years covers a period of rapid physical development. It is the time for the formation of the sense activities as related to the intellect. The child in this age develops his senses. His attention is further attracted to the environment under the form of passive curiosity . . . The development of the senses indeed precedes that of superior intellectual activity and the child between three and seven years is in the period of formation. (MM, 215–216).

The education of the senses makes men observers. (MM, 218) . . . In a pedagogical method which is experimental the education of the senses must undoubtedly assume the greatest importance . . . The education of the senses has, as its aim, the refinement of the differential perception of stimuli by means of repeated exercises. (MM, 167–173) . . . The senses are points of contact with the environment . . . The child who has worked with our sensorial apparatus has not only acquired greater skill in the use of his hands, but has also achieved a higher degree of perceptiveness towards those stimuli which come to him from the outside world . . . Our sensorial material provides a kind of guide to observation, for it classifies the impressions that each sense can receive . . . The senses being explorers of the world, open the way to knowledge. Our apparatus for educating the senses offers the child a key to guide his exploration of the world, they cast a light upon it which makes visible to him more things in greater detail than he could see in the dark, or uneducated state. (AM, 182–183)

It is exactly in the repetition of the exercises that the education of the senses consists; their aim is not that the child shall *know* colors, forms and the different qualities of objects, but that he refine his senses through an exercise of attention, of comparison, of judgment. (MM, 360) . . . For the education of the senses in general, such as in the tactile, thermic, baric, and steriognostic exercises, we blindfold the children . . . the blindfold greatly increases their interest, without making the exercise degenerate into noisy fun . . . They are very proud of *seeing without their eyes*. (MM, 179 & 190)

Another important particular in the technique of sense education lies in *isolating the sense*, whenever this is possible . . . one should proceed from *few stimuli strongly contrasting, to many stimuli in gradual differentiation always more fine and imperceptible*. (MM, 179–184)

The education of the tactile and the thermic senses go together . . . The limitation of the exercises of the tactile sense to the cushioned tips of the fingers, is rendered necessary by practical life. It must be made a necessary phase of *education* because it prepares for a life in which man exercises and uses the tactile sense through the medium of these fingertips . . . I next teach the child how to *touch*, that is, the manner in which he should touch surfaces. For this it is necessary to take the finger of the child and to draw it *very, very lightly over the surface* . . . Another particular of the technique is to teach the child to hold his eyes closed while he touches, encouraging him to do this by telling him that he will be able to feel the differences better, and so leading him to distinguish, without the help of sight, the change of contact. (MM, 185–186)

The olfactory sense in children is not developed to any great extent, and this makes it difficult to attract their attention by means of the senses. (MM, 190)

Beauty lies in harmony, not in contrast; and harmony is refinement; therefore, there must be a fineness of the senses if we are to appreciate harmony. (MM, 222)

Language

The learning of language is truly the child's most remarkable intellectual achievement, and yet it is accomplished rapidly in a very short time span. Ideally, the parents, who are the child's first language teachers, should begin during his early infancy to give verbal meaning to the things in the child's environment. Montessori's own comments on language deal largely with complex terminology regarding the mechanism of language pertaining to the nervous system. For those with a special interest, extensive explanation of this can be found in *The Montessori Method and the Absorbent Mind*. For the layman, it is enough to know that vocabulary building takes place daily, and many varied language experiences are needed to build and enrich the child's foundation for learning to read and write. Language is an integral part of the Montessori classroom, through encouragement of self-expression, lessons, and freedom of conversation.

Languages absorbed in early childhood are evident and inimitable. They are our "mother-tongue." They are the property of the ignorant as well as of the learned . . . By merely "living" and without any conscious effort the individual absorbs from the environment even a complex cultural achievement like language. (CE, 82–89)

Language lies at the root of that transformation of the environment that we all call civilization . . . Language is an instrument of *collective thoughts* . . . and grows with human thought. (AM, 108–109) . . . The child of six who has learned to speak correctly, knowing and using the rules of his native tongue, could never describe the unconscious work from which all this has come. Nevertheless, it is he, *man*, who is the creator of speech. (AM, 115)

Writing and Reading

. . . writing precedes reading . . . we do not need to *teach* writing. The child who draws, will write . . . I was struck by an idea which had never before entered my mind—that in writing we make *two diverse* forms of movement, for, besides the movement by which the form is reproduced, there is also that of *manipulating the instrument of writing* . . . Writing is very quickly learned, because we begin to teach it only to those children who show a desire for it by spontaneous attention to the lesson given by the directress to other children, or by watching the exercises in which the others are occupied. Some individuals *learn* without ever having received any lessons, solely through listening to the lessons given to others. (MM, 262–293)

The average time that elapses between the first trial of the preparatory exercises and the first written word is, for children of four years, from a month to a month and a half. The first word written by my little ones arouse within themselves an indescribable emotion of joy. (MM, 288–294)

Progress in writing is marked by the parallel development of the written and spoken language. (S, 160) . . . the child's explosion into writing is closely connected with his special sensitivity for language, and this was operative at the time when he began to speak. By the age of five and a half or six this sensitivity has ceased to exist; so it is clear that writing can be learned with joy and enthusiasm only before that age . . . we know from other experiences that this easy writing does not come from our use of the sensitive period alone: it also depends on certain preparatory exercises which the child does at an earlier stage still, when his hand is busy with our carefully designed apparatus for practicing his powers of sensorial discrimination. (AM, 173)

Our children have long been preparing the hand for writing. Throughout all the sensory exercises the hand, whilst cooperating with the mind in its attainments and in its work of formation, was preparing its own future . . . the child is taught to pass the soft cushioned tips of his fingers as lightly as possible . . . (H, 77) . . . Tracing the letter, in the fashion of writing, begins the muscular education which prepares for writing . . . As for the touching of the letters, I thought of cutting the letters of the alphabet out of sandpaper and of gluing them upon smooth cards, thus making objects much like those used in the primitive exercises for the tactile sense . . . Corresponding to each letter of the alphabet, we had a picture representing some object the name of which began with the letter. (MM, 262–269) . . . Whilst the child touches a letter, the teacher pronounces its sound. (H, 152)

We have . . . begun the teaching of *reading* at the same time that we have been teaching writing. When we present a letter to the child and enunciate its sound, he fixes the image of this letter by means of the visual sense . . . when he sees and recognizes, he reads, and when he traces, he writes.

The letters of the alphabet used . . . are cut out of cardboard

. . . the vowels are cut from blue cardboard, and the consonants from red . . . The directress pronounces *very* clearly a word . . . repeating the sounds a number of times . . . The child selects (the vowel) then composes the other syllables . . . once he has understood the mechanism of the game, the child goes forward by himself, and becomes intensely interested. We may pronounce any word, taking care only that the child understands separately the letters of which it is composed . . . The importance of these exercises is very complex. The child analyzes, perfects, fixes his own spoken language, placing an object in correspondence to every sound heard with the graphic sign which represents it, and lays a most solid foundation for accurate and perfect spelling . . . When the child hears others read the word he has composed, he wears an expression of satisfaction and pride, and is possessed by a species of joyous wonder. He is impressed by this correspondence, carried on between himself and others by means of symbols. (MM, 280–290)

I do not consider as *reading* the test which the child makes when he verifies the word that he has written . . . What I understand by reading is the *interpretation* of an idea from the written signs . . . writing aids the physiological language and reading aids the social language . . . We begin then with . . . the reading of names of objects which are well known or present . . . I understood that the time had come when we might proceed to the reading of phrases . . . Reading, if it is to teach the child to receive an idea, should be mental and not vocal. (MM, 301)

We do not trouble ourselves as to whether the child in the development of this process, first learns to read or to write, or if the one or the other will be the easier. We must rid ourselves of all preconceptions, and must *await from experience* the answer to these questions. We may expect that individual differences will show themselves in the prevalence of one or the other act in the development of different children. (MM, 281)

Arithmetic

Sensorial training is of great importance in learning the basics of arithmetic. Montessori has a wide variety of materials for this purpose, thus allowing the child to become familiar with numbers at an early age. The idea of quantity is inherent in all the Montessori arithmetic materials and the conception of identity and difference in the sensorial exercises is built up from recognition of identical objects and gradation of similar ones.

The young child is enabled, through repeated work with the materials, sandpaper numbers, rods, spindle box, etc, to learn the names of the numbers before grasping the abstract conceptions.

The children possess all the instinctive knowledge necessary as a preparation for clear ideas on numeration. The idea of quantity was inherent in all the material for the education of the senses . . . The child's mind is . . . prepared for number . . . by a process of formation, by a slow building up of itself . . . When we begin the direct teaching of number, we choose the long rods, dividing them into ten spaces, colored alternately red and blue. When the rods have been placed in order of gradation we teach the child the numbers . . . and the lesson in three periods . . . The teaching of the actual figures marks an advance from the rods to the process of counting with separate units. When the figures are known, they will serve the very purpose in the abstract which the rods serve in the concrete. (H, 164–174)

Imagination and Fantasy

Critics of the method steadfastly maintain that Montessori was an opponent of fantasy, that she excluded make-believe from her classrooms and would not permit the children to read fairy tales. Admittedly, some of her writings become extremely complex on the subject, particularly when dealing with the spiritual aspects of fantasy, so that the lay reader could easily misinterpret her feelings. Progressive educators of her day, as well as the Froebelians, placed strong emphasis on fantasy play in early childhood, making her ideas alien to those already established. Even today many Montessori pre-schools use "Let's Pretend." I feel that this is done primarily as a diversion, because they don't feel that young children are ready for more cognitive learning experiences.

To understand Montessori's feelings on imagination, it is first necessary to know how she defined it. She felt that imagination developed from impressions within the environment and was based on truth. To her it was a means for encouraging the child to use his brain in a creative way, when based on realistic contact with life rather than on childhood fantasy and speculation. Increased competency in accurate perception of things in the prepared environment prepared the child for understanding imaginative thought, and thus imagination was developed from reality impressions within this environment.

Imagination can have only a sensory basis . . . If then, the true basis of the imagination is reality, and its perception is related to exactness of observation, it is necessary to prepare children to perceive the things in their environment exactly, in order to secure for them the material required by the imagination . . . It is from freedom of development that we may expect the manifestations of his imagination.

A form of imagination supposed to be "proper" to childhood, and almost universally recognized as creative imagination, is that spontaneous work of the infant mind by which children attribute desirable characteristics to objects which do not possess them. (SAE, 248–264)

Normally, objects used by children, in fantasy express the contents of a child's own experience and act as a sign indicating the transition between fantsay and reality, while maintaining a connection between the two. The child makes those objects around him fit into his fantasy world through imaginative use. It is easier for the young child to relate to reality because it's something tangible and concrete. Montessori observed that children, given the choice, preferred activities relating to the environment around them: reality-oriented, objects and actions. Within the Montessori classroom, the children working in practical-life activities, for example, are basing their actions on those of the adults in their environment. In a sense, this is meeting their need for fantasy or dramatic play; they are imitating the functions of others in a reality-oriented situation. They often also attempt to escape to a make-believe world from a "real world" created for them by adults.

Children who are lonely or without the activity necessary for their developing minds and bodies will often withdraw to a fantasy world as an escape. Depending upon the extent of their emotions this can be a means of temporary comfort or an unhealthy sign. The danger comes when one is unable to distinguish fantasy from reality. The young child has a tendency to dwell on fantasies that he creates, but the normal child readily recognizes this distinction.

Another feature that always accompanies . . . disorder . . . is the child's difficulty, or inability, to concentrate his attention on real objects. His mind prefers to wander in the realm of fantasy. While playing games with stones or dried leaves, he talks as if he were preparing delicious banquets on immense tables, and his imagination will probably take the most extravagant forms when he grows up. The more the mind is divorced from its normal function, the more exhausted it becomes, and useless as a servant of the spirit, which needs to have as its goal the development of the inner life . . . The wandering mind that breaks away from reality, breaks away also from healthy normality. In the world of fantasy, wherein it thrives, there is no control of error, nothing to coordinate thought . . . (AM, 266)

We have all seen children expressing vivid imagination and often marveled at their gifts. Personally I do not consider this a detriment and feel that it is not too difficult to know when the child has left the realm of reality and is experiencing abnormal behavior. Healthy imagination does not mean that the child will grow up to be a demented adult. It is the circumstances which are important. Given the scope of educating the *whole* personality of the child, fantasy takes a relative position in perspective to the many other areas of development which constitute the method.

Montessori believed the theory that the young child not only couldn't relate to the fantasy involved in fairy tales, but didn't need them, as real life was interesting enough to him at this stage of limited experience. Fairy tales are indeed a part of the Montessori classroom, but they are clearly defined as such.

Drama itself was something that Montessori used freely as a learning tool. For example, by means of the command cards of forming sentences, children would be asked to act out messages extemporaneously: "Doug went to the window and opened it," "Sarah sat on the chair and cried," "Jennifer jumped for joy." In the upper grades of the European Montessori schools, students write and produce plays, and in America I've seen pre-schoolers act out rhymes and stories, while older children recite verses and perform in plays. It should be remembered, too, that the very writing of compositions is a means of imagination and expressing one's self.

Art and Music

Montessori gave no specific instructions, as such, in art and drawing. Instead she laid a foundation enabling the child to be successful by his own spontaneous initiative. The sensorial exercises prepared the hand for writing and, later, drawing. Such exercises as outlining geometric figures and filling them in with careful strokes of a colored pencil may seem too rigid a restriction for the young child. The purpose, however, is not to provide him with free expression of art, but to train his eye and hand for this eventual task. Everywhere in the prepared environment, the child is exposed to color, form, and beauty, helping him to develop his awareness, aesthetic sense and artistic appreciation, and a later spontaneous interest in art. This indirect approach leads to increased creativity and freedom of exploration and expression.

The so-called "free drawing" has no place in my system. I avoid those useless, immature, weary efforts and those frightful drawings that are so popular in "advanced" schools today . . . We do not give lessons in drawing or in modeling, and yet many of our children know how to draw flowers, birds, landscapes, and even imaginary scenes in an admirable way . . . We do not teach a child to draw by having him draw, but by giving him the opportunity to prepare his means of expression . . . I consider this to be a great aid to free drawing since, being neither inefficacious nor incomprehensible, it encourages a child to continue . . . We might note in conclusion that the best way to teach drawing is not to leave a child completely free, but to provide the means for its natural development by training the hand. True talent will spontaneously manifest itself. (D, 308–309)

The young child is only capable of an introduction to music and its appreciation. His environment should contain objects that will arouse his feelings and understanding for music. Initially, good music is introduced, then rhythmic exercises involving motor skills and exercises for interpreting and comparing and contrasting different rhythms. Harmony and melody are introduced, and suitable children's instruments are used. Later the bells and musical notes are included.

The technique for the education of music consists in picking out a single musical phrase that can be easily interpreted and playing it over and over again . . . Music must be played exactly and with feeling, that is, it must be played and interpreted musically . . . The precise way in which a child comes to mark the tempo of a musical beat without having been taught the division into three-fourths and four-fourths time is a proof of the sense education derived from musical rhythms. (D, 313)

Physical Education and Nature

Montessori felt that gymnastics programs in the regular schools were inadequate, and she objected to the disciplined regimen used in presenting it to children. She felt that this repressed their spontaneous movements.

We must understand by *gymnastics* and in general by muscular education a series of exercises teaching to *aid* the normal development (such as walking, breathing, speech), to protect this development, when the child shows himself backward or abnormal in any way, and to encourage in the children those movements which are useful in the achievement of the most ordinary acts of life; such as dressing, undressing, buttoning their clothes, and lacing their shoes, carrying such objects as balls, cubes, etc. If there exists an age in which it is necessary to protect a child by means of a series of gymnastic exercises, between three and six years is undoubtedly the age. (MM, 130)

Montessori made intricate studies of the relative proportions of the child's body and its growth, and determined the torso to be far more developed as compared to the limbs, which are also short in comparison.

Now we, with the gymnastics, can, and indeed, should, help the child in his development by making our exercises correspond to the movements which he needs to make and in this way save his limbs from fatigue. (D, 135) . . . Of itself, movement is something unrefined, but its true success increases when one attempts to perfect it. (D, 90)

Once again, through observation, Montessori worked out various exercises to aid the children in muscular control and coordination of movements, while exercising different parts of the body. There were also "free" gymnastics, the normal childhood games played with balls, hoops, bean bags, etcetera, and preferably done outdoors to take advantage of the fresh air. She felt that exercises pertaining to correct carriage, the respiratory system, speech habits, and exercises for the fingers were all of equal importance. Naturally, the exercises for practical life and the sensory materials aided her plan for muscular education.

The educational value of a movement depends on the finality of the movement; and it must be such that it helps the child to perfect something in himself; either it perfects the voluntary mucular system; or some mental capacity; or both. Educational movement must always be an activity which builds up and fortifies the personality, giving him a new power and not leaving him where he was. . . . (D, 142)

Physical education was an integral part of developing the total child. Apart from gymnastics it also emphasized the hygienic aspect of fresh air, through visits to the park or beach and walks within the city. Not restricting the child's movements with excessive clothing was something that Montessori also stressed. I was reminded of this on a tour of schools in the U.S.S.R. It was summertime and most of the activities took place outdoors. The children up to age seven wore only underpants, and the infants, diapers, but they all wore hats to protect them from the sun, they also spent much time preparing the soil—planting, tending, then harvesting crops of flowers, vegetables, and fruit. Montessori students in the Children's House have also done this. This led to a spontaneous and purposeful exploration of nature and also involved detailed studies of plant and animal life, ecology, and the relationship of man to his environment.

ON EDUCATION AND SCHOOLS

. . . any reform of education must be based on the personality of man. Man himself must become the center of education and we must never forget that man does not develop only at the university, but begins his mental growth at birth, and pursues it with the greatest intensity during the first three years of his life. (AM, 8) . . . By education must be understood the active *help* given to the normal expansion of the life of the child. (MM, 104) . . . an educational method, which cultivates and protects the inner activities of the child, is not a question which concerns merely the school or the teachers; it is a universal question which concerns the family, and is of vital interest to mothers. (H, 185)

The education of our day is rich in methods, aims and social ends, but one must still say that it takes no account of life itself . . . Education, as today conceived, is something separated both from biological and social life. (AM, 10) . . . I personally believe that we should give more intention to imparting a *spirit* to teachers than scientific techniques, that is, our aim should be towards what is intellectual rather than material . . . One who desires to be a teacher must have an interest in humanity that connects the observer with the observed more closely than that which joins the zoologist or biologist to nature; . . . (D, 5–8) . . . if we wish to conduct educational experiments, we must not have recourse to kindred sciences, but must free our minds so that they can proceed without hindrance in their search for the truths that belong properly and exclusively to teaching. We must not therefore start from any fixed ideas about child psychology but with a program that will give a child his freedom so that we can deduce a truly scientific child psychology by observing his spontaneous reactions. It may well be that such a program holds great surprises in store for us. (D, 20)

The most urgent task facing educators is to come to know this unknown child and to free it from all entanglements. (S, 134) . . . It behooves us to think of what may happen to the *spirit* of the child who is condemned to grow in conditions so artificial that his very bones may become deformed. (MM, 20) . . . Today we hold the pupils in school, restricted by those instruments so degrading to body and spirit, the desk and material prizes and punishments. Our aim in all this is to reduce them to the discipline of immobility and silence,—to lead them,—where? Far too often toward no definite end. Often the education of children consists in pouring into their intelligence the intellectual contents of school programs. And often these programs have been compiled in the official department of education, and their use is imposed by law upon the teacher and the child. (MM, 26–27) . . . What the schools need is more liberty, not such a contraption as a desk. (D, 130)

The transformation of the school must be contemporaneous with the preparation of the teacher. For if we make of the teacher an observer, familiar with the experimental methods, then we must make it possible for her to observe and to experiment in the school. The fundamental principle of scientific pedagogy must be, indeed, the *liberty of the pupil*; such liberty as shall permit a development of individual, spontaneous manifestations of the child's nature. If a new and scientific pedagogy is to arise from the *study of the individual*, such study must occupy itself with the observation of *free* children . . . we must proceed by a method which shall tend to make possible to the child complete liberty . . . Child psychology and pedagogy must establish their content by successive conquests arrived at through the method of experimentation. (MM, 20–28)

My vision of the future is no longer of people taking exams and proceeding on that certification from the secondary school to the university, but of individuals passing from one stage of independence to a higher, by means of their own activity, through their own effort of will, which constitutes the inner evolution of the individual. (CA, Intro.)

7. Appendixes

A. FAMILIAR MONTESSORI TERMS

Absorbent mind The ability and ease with which the young child learns, unconsciously, from his environment.

Casa de Bambini "Children's House," or "House of Childhood"; this was the name given the first schools using the Montessori method.

Control of error The possibility inherent in the Montessori materials of making apparent the mistakes made by the child, thereby allowing him to see his errors after completing the exercises and to correct them.

Cosmic education The attempt through use of the sensitive periods, to give the child the help needed to develop himself as a total being.

Cosmic task To continue the work of creation by maintaining the environment to support future generations of all living species.

Cycles of activity These periods of concentration on a particular task that should be worked to completion.

Deviated Child The child who has not yet found himself and thus is restless and difficult to control. He finds adjustment difficult and often escapes into a fantasy world.

Didactic materials The instructive materials used by the child for self-teaching.

Directress The name for the teacher in a Montessori school, who acts as observer and director of the child's learning activities.

Discovery of the child. Dr. Montessori's awareness and realization of the young child as an "unknown entity" who manifests himself spontaneously in the present moment.

Explosion into learning The continuous, intense application to one kind of work exclusively for a period of time.

Formative years The years from birth to six when the child is forming his personality.

Freedom The child's free movements and experiences in an environment that provides discipline through liberty and respect for his rights.

Independence The overcoming of obstacles and dependence on others in his attempt to gain freedom and self-development.

Inner guide That which enables the child to choose that work which will best assist his development.

Isolation of difficulty The concentration of one particular aspect of a task or exercise in order to better understand it.

Liberty The opportunity for activity within an educational framework of structure and discipline.

Normalized child The child who expresses his true nature in complete harmony with his environment; loving order and constructive activity; precociously intelligent, self-disciplined, and joyfully sympathetic to others.

Order The giving of a specific time, location and meaning to everything in the environment to help the child establish order in his mind and in his learning habits.

Practical life exercises Those exercises through which the child learns to care for himself and his environment.

Prepared environment An atmosphere created to enable the child to be free to learn through his own activity in peaceful and orderly surroundings adapted to the child's size and interests.

Psychic embryo Those inherent patterns of mental functions.

<u>*Sensitive periods*</u> Those periods of learning (to walk, talk, write, et cetera) during which a child is particularly sensitive to a specific stimulus.

Sensorial exercises Those exercises pertaining to the development of the five senses and to providing a foundation for speech, writing, and arithmetic by use of the sensorial materials.

Sensorial materials The Montessori equipment designed to teach the child by means of focusing the mind on specific sensory responses.

Spiritual embryo The newborn child with his potentials for developing into a spiritual man.

B. CLASSROOM MATERIALS

MOTOR EDUCATION
Practical Life Exercises
Dressing Frames
Polishing Shoes
Washing Hands
Pouring Rice/Water
Sweeping, Dusting, Folding
Setting Table
Sorting, Twisting
Scrubbing, Peeling, Polishing
Washing and Drying Dishes and Hands
Cutting and Pasting
Walking a Line

SENSORY EDUCATION
Tactile
Rough and Smooth Boards
Fabrics
Mystery Bag
Baric Tablets
Thermal Bottles

Visual
  Knobbed Cylinders
  Knobless Cylinders
  Pink Tower
  Brown Stair
  Long Rods
  Color Tablets
  Geometric Cabinet
  Geometric Solids
  Constructive Triangles
  Binomial and Trinomial Cubes
Auditory
  Sound Cylinders
  Bells
  Silence Game
Gustatory
  Tasting Bottles
Olfactory
  Smell Bottles

LANGUAGE
  Sandpaper Letters
  Metal Insets
  Movable Alphabet
  Phonetic Words
  Initial Consonants
  Object and Words
  Phonogram Booklets
  Parts of Speech
  Singular and Plural
  Positive, Comparative, Superlative
  Grammar Symbols

ARITHMETIC
  Number Rods
  Sandpaper Numbers
  Spindle Box
  Golden Bead Material
  Bead Frames
  Fraction Insets

Sequin Boards
Charts and Boards for Addition, Subtraction, Multiplication,
and Division

Dr. Montessori, in *Dr. Montessori's Own Handbook*, pp. 51–53,
describes the following:

The Didactic Material for the Education of the Senses Consists of:
   a) Three sets of solid insets.
   b) Three sets of solids in graduated sizes, comprising:
      1) Pink cubes.
      2) Brown prisms.
      3) Rods: a) colored green; b) colored alternately red and
         blue.
   c) Various geometric solids (prism, pyramid, sphere, cylin-
      der, cone, etc.)
   d) Rectangular tablets with rough and smooth surfaces.
   e) A collection of various stuffs.
   f) Small wooden tablets of different weights.
   g) Two boxes, each containing sixty-four colored tablets.
   h) A chest of drawers containing plane insets.
   i) Three series of cards on which are pasted geometrical
      forms in paper.
      *
   k) A collection of cylindrical closed boxes (sounds).
   l) A double series of musical bells, wooden boards on which
      are painted the lines used in music, small wooden discs
      for the notes.
         *Note: j) is omitted in the book

The Didactic Material for the Preparation for Writing and
Arithmetic
   m) Two sloping desks and various iron insets.
   n) Cards on which are pasted sandpaper letters.
   o) Two alphabets of colored cardboard and of different
      sizes.
   p) A series of cards on which are pasted sandpaper figures
      (1, 2, 3, etc.).

q) A series of large cards bearing the same figures in smooth paper for the numeration of numbers above ten.
r) Two boxes with small sticks for counting.
s) The volume of drawings belonging specifically to the method, and colored pencils.
t) The frames for lacing, buttoning, etc., which are used for the education of the movements of the hand.

Muscular education has reference to:
The primary movements of everyday life (walking, rising, sitting, handling objects).
The care of the person.
Management of the household.
Gardening.
Manual work.
Gymnastic exercises.
Rhythmic movements.

C. A COMPARISON OF MONTESSORI AND TRADITIONAL PRE-SCHOOL EDUCATION

MONTESSORI	TRADITIONAL
three-year age span	all one age
motivated by self-development	teacher-motivated
ungraded	graded
self-correcting materials	teacher corrects errors
children learn by handling objects and teaching themselves	teacher lectures
individual learning	group learning
teacher is observer and directress	teacher is focal point and dominant influence
child completes "cycles of activity"	activity cycles determined by set time
few interruptions	frequent interruptions
freedom to move and work within classroom	assigned seats and specific class periods
emphasis on more cognitive learning	postponement of 3R's, emphasis on social development

quiet by choice and out of regard for others	quiet enforced
materials used for specific purpose with sequence of steps	materials used in many ways without previous instruction
work for joy of working and sense of discovery	work because they're told to
environment provides discipline	teacher provides discipline
encouraged to help one another	seek help from teacher
child chooses materials	teacher sets curriculum
child sets own pace	teacher sets pace
child free to discover on own	teacher guides child
emphasis on concrete	emphasis on abstract
reality-oriented	much role-playing and fantasy
specific places for materials, sense of order	random placement, not necessary to return to specific place
child provides own stimulus to learning	teacher provides
child-centered learning environment	teacher-centered
self-education through self-correcting materials	use of reward and punishment in motivation
recognition of sensitive periods	all children treated alike
multisensory materials to develop specific skills	play materials for nonspecific skills

D. CHOOSING A MONTESSORI SCHOOL FOR YOUR CHILD

Five essential features of an effective Montessori school are: philosophy, personnel, physical plant, program, and pupils. A school should be judged by these features and the school's commitment to three Montessori principles: observation, individual liberty, and preparation of the environment. If you want a Montessori education for your child, you must first have done enough reading on the subject to know how your own philosophy of child-rearing and education compare and differ from that offered in a Montessori school. Before going to observe schools, set up a mental list of your criteria and know exactly what it is that you're looking for to suit best the needs of your child. It is important to find a school atmosphere compatible with the home environment, rather than one diametrically opposed to it. Children learn far more from imitation of what they see and do, rather than from what they hear.

Because of individual adaptations and interpretations, all Montessori schools differ somewhat. These differences can be minor or significant, but there will always be some common elements.

You will find an environment prepared with child-size furnishings, an array of learning apparatus on shelves, children free to move about while pursuing disciplined activity, working singly or in small groups usually within a three-year span. The teachers should be observing and directing the activities of the children. Most important to you as a parent should be the attitude of the children and teachers you observe and their interaction and rapport with each other. Remember that any classroom can have an impressive array of materials and the superficial appearance of a "good school," but there's far more to be observed than just that.

You want a place where your child will feel happy and secure while he's learning, a place where he is treated and respected as an individual and where he feels comfortable in his surroundings, while realizing what is expected of him in this new situation. A child's first school experience has a great effect on his future feelings concerning school and the learning process, and it is vitally important to make a wise decision affecting these early stages of development.

What Montessori can do for your child will largely depend on how his directress interprets and applies the Dottoressa's philosophy and principles in a concrete situation. The biggest favor that you can do your child, once he has been enrolled in a Montessori school, is to become actively involved yourself also. It is a total commitment to Montessori principles that guides his life and development. Most Montessori schools conduct an active parent-education program to guide parents in a better understanding of the method and the role of school and home. All parents need background in the method, since it is important for it to carry over from school to home.

On a national average, the annual tuition for a Montessori school is $650. This can vary, depending on the program. Some operate three days a week, others five; some offer half-day programs, while others are full-day. The general annual price range is $400–$1200. Of course there are many federally funded or church-based programs which cost considerably less. Check your own particular locale for what's available.

The age groupings are: three-, four- and five-year-olds for preschool, and six-, seven- and eight-year-olds grouped together for primary grades. This too can differ from school to school. Many schools insist on a five-day-a-week program for all ages. I personally consider this to be too much for the young child, who should be spending most of his time with his mother. For the working mother, an all-day program would be a better alternative than leaving the child with a babysitter.

E. THE FOUNDING OF THE AMERICAN MONTESSORI SOCIETY (A.M.S.)

In 1960, Nancy McCormick Rambusch discussed the reintroduction of the Montessori method into the United States with Mario Montessori, who as the head of Association Montessori Internationale (A.M.I.) was its sole policymaker. As the timing appeared to be right, he expressed interest and appointed Mrs. Rambusch the A.M.I. representative. Thus began several years of negotiation and work in an attempt to affiliate A.M.I. and A.M.S. It was important for A.M.S. to adapt Montessori to its own country's needs and culture and to set standards accordingly—in effect, to "Americanize" Montessori and make it relevant.

A great deal of thought and discussion went into teacher-training courses, interpretation of doctrine, and discussion of what the exact relationship beween A.M.S. and A.M.I. should be. Predictably, differences arose. In 1963, A.M.I. severed their association with A.M.S., but remained on amicable terms.

A.M.I. is now represented in the United States by the Washington Montessori Institute, and has eight other training centers throughout the United States. A.M.S. continues to represent itself as the "Americanization" of Montessori.

The founding, by Lee Havis, of the International Montessori Society in the United States in 1979, added a new dimension to the Montessori community. Its purpose was to support the effective application of Montessori principles throughout the world. The Society (I.M.S.) defines Montessori as a commitment to three fundamental principles: (1) "observation," (2) "individual liberty," and (3) "preparation of the environment." It asserts that only a complete commitment to these three principles with children will assure the emergence of the "normalized" child as intended by Dr. Montessori. This assertion challenges the popular interpretations of Montessori as a rationale or "philosophy" limited to teaching techniques involving specific materials. The I.M.S. identifies itself with "that which is creating Dr. Montessori's vision of a 'new education' . . . to free children from all forms of adult tyranny."

Numerous other separatist groups have formed, offering their own interpretations of the Montessori doctrine. All of these groups have played a role in gaining a wider acceptance of Montessori education in America.

F. MONTESSORI INFORMATIONAL SOURCES

NOTE: There are many companies trying to benefit from the fact that Montessori is a generic term and in the public domain. The result is a profusion of books, materials, schools, and training programs which may complicate an intelligent inquiry into the field. Rather than list everything that is available, I have selected those sources most widely recognized today. Exclusion of some does not necessarily indicate their lack of constructive contribution to the work of Montessori, but rather is an accommodation to space and clarity.

Organizations

THE AMERICAN MONTESSORI SOCIETY (A.M.S.), 150 Fifth Avenue, New York, NY 10011, was formed in 1960 to promote better education for all children through use of the Montessori method and its incorporation into American education. It is a national, nonprofit, tax-exempt, self-supporting membership organization, comprised of parents, teachers, administrators, and educators. Society policy is made by a board of not more than twelve Directors and administrated by a National Director. Its main purpose is to act as a clearinghouse for information and data on Montessori education, organize teacher-training courses and workshops, and provide consultation services and resource materials for affiliates. It also provides numerous A.M.S. publications and lists of source material, considering an "open minded attitude" and "respect for the child . . . the most fundamental aspect of Montessori education."

THE ASSOCIATION MONTESSORI INTERNATIONALE, (A.M.I.), 161 Koninginneweg, Amsterdam, Holland, (A.M.I.-U.S.A., 7211 Regency Square Blvd., Suite 215, Houston, TX 77036), was established in 1929 by Dr. Maria Montessori and was directed by her son, Mario Montessori, until his death in 1982. This organization considers itself to be the international authority on Montessori education. It views Monessori as a "complex of philosophy, psychology, educational theory, materials and methods." It works to retain the original purist application of Dr. Montessori's philsophy and teaching methods.

THE INTERNATIONAL MONTESSORI SOCIETY (I.M.S.), 912 Thayer Avenue, Silver Spring, MD 20910, was established in 1979 by Lee Havis. It is a nonprofit, tax-exempt organization with international membership consisting of parents, teachers, and other interested individuals and organizations. Montessori school membership is based on an expressed commitment to Montessori principles as set forth in specific written criteria. The Society offers publications, consultation, teacher training, and other such support services on behalf of Montessori education, while providing "the structural network for individuals and schools to participate effectively in the work of creating the 'new education.' "

NATIONAL CENTER FOR MONTESSORI EDUCATION (N.C.M.E.) 4544 Pocahontas Ave., San Diego, CA 92117, was founded by Dennis A. Laskin in 1977 and presently operates as a nonprofit corporation registered in the state of California. A board of directors oversees its operation and determines policy. It offers affiliation for teacher-training centers, workshops, publications, and other such programs relative to Montessori education. It refers to Montessori as a "method and philosophy."

MONTESSORI INSTITUTE OF AMERICA (M.I.A.), 3550 Galt Ocean Drive, Fort Lauderdale, FL 33308, was founded as a nonprofit organization in 1971 by Dr. Helen K. Billings, as a means of promoting the method as a solution to the problems facing American education. A Board of Directors oversees the running of teacher-training programs, workshops, and conferences, while sharing the common goal of promoting the Montessori movement in America. Membership is open to all who share these goals.

Other Sources

There are numerous Montessori societies in states and cities throughout the United States. Most have been formed by interested parents to promote and disseminate information regarding the Montessori method through means of study groups, newsletters, and workshops. For a local society in your area, consult the telephone directory or inquire at a Montessori school. If nothing is available and there is interest, contact one of the organizations listed above that seems to match your own goals and purpose about starting one.

Materials

The teaching materials designed by Maria Montessori have proven most beneficial in the "self education" of the child. Through manipulation of these specially designed learning tools the young child teaches himself in accordance with his internal and external development. Although each piece of apparatus contains within it a correction of error, enabling the child to work by himself and at his own rate, it must nevertheless be remembered that these tools are of little value if not properly presented to the child before he begins to explore their use. Correct parent or teacher training in the understanding, use, and presentation of the materials is imperative. (*Teaching Montessori in the Home: The Pre-School Years*

and *Teaching Montessori in the Home: The School Years*, both by
Elizabeth G. Hainstock, may be useful guides for parents).

Firms selling Montessori Teaching Materials
United States

Albanesi Educational Center
4331 Allencrest Lane
Dallas, TX 75244

El Paso Montessori Suppliers
3109 Dyer Street
El Paso, TX 79930

Kaybee Montessori
4717 Chesapeake ST. N.W.
Washington, DC 20016

Montessori Matters and E-Z Learning Material
701 East Columbia Avenue
Cincinnati, OH 45215

Montessori Services
816 King Street
Santa Rosa, CA 95405

Montessori Shop/Michael Olaf
5655 Keith Avenue
Oakland, CA 94618

Nienhuis Montessori USA
320 Pioneer Way
Mt. View, CA 94041

Southwest Montessori Training Center
P.O. Box 13466-N. Texas Station
Denton, TX 76203

Success Research Consultants
1439 Monroe
River Forest, IL 60610

Yankee Montessori Manufacturing
8655 South Amin
Los Angeles, CA 90003-3499

Foreign

England: St. Nicholas Training Center
    23 Princess Gate
    London, SW7, England

Holland: A. Nienhuis Montessori
    14 Industripark
    Zelham, Holland

India: Kaybee International
    75-B Patharia Palace
    Mohammedali Road
    Bombay 400 003 India

Italy: C. Baroni and G. Manangon
    46023 Gonzaga
    Montova, Italy

Selected catalogs for supplemental materials (some including Montessori) can be obtained from:

Childcraft
20 Kilmer Road
Edison, N.J. 08818

Educational Teaching Aids
159 West Kinzie
Chicago, IL 60610

Lakeshore Curriculum Materials Co.
2695 E. Dominguez Street
Carson, CA 90749

Philip and Tacey, Ltd
69-79 Fulham High Street
London, SW6, England

Toys To Grow On
P.O. Box 17
Long Beach, CA 90801

G. MONTESSORI TEACHER-TRAINING PROGRAMS

Offered for over two decades in the United States Montessori teacher-training has become increasingly available in recent years, providing a diverse range of programs. Many lead to a diploma or certificate based on quite different formats, standards, and contents. Indeed, the nature and substance of preparation from one course to another as diverse as are the range of opinions and interpretations of Montessori itself.

Because there is presently no single comprehensive accrediting agency to set uniform minimum standards or to otherwise qualify institutions issuing a Montessori certificate, possession of such a certificate does not necessarily assure a definitive level of course work completion. A Montessori certificate is therefore no guarantee of employment nor is it necessarily an assurance of having met minimum staff training requirements as required by government regulation employed in the operation of Montessori schools.

Many years ago, as Montessori was beginning its regrowth in the United States, the only recognized diplomas were issued by A.M.S. and A.M.I. Currently the value and use of any particular Montessori certificate is also necessarily subject to the authority and position of the issuing entity. Since 1967, many diverse organizations and teacher-training institutions have emerged to employ freely the "Montessori" label in their title—each issuing their own brand of certification based on their own criteria or interpretation of Montessori. In *American Montessori Society, Inc. v. Association Montessori Internationale,* (155 U.S.P.Q. 591,592 (1967), the U.S. Patent and Trademark Trial and Appeal Board refused to grant exclusive use of the term *Montessori* to one particular "Montessori" organization because "the term *Montessori* has a generic and/or descriptive significance."

Ultimately, each individual must answer for himself the question "what is Montessori?" and decide which training program will teach the desired method and satisfy individual needs. For anyone wishing to start a school or become a full-time director, self-preparation is vital. Effective preparation in this regard is not readily measurable in distinctions of training programs, or in terms of length and number of lectures, practice sessions, use of materials, and practical internship experience. Rather, the program's view and approaches to Montessori itself are foremost in importance for consideration.

A Montessori certificate is not a guarantee of employment and many Montessori schools prefer that an applicant be trained in a way specifically suitable to their own establishment. Individuals interested in becoming Montessori teachers should contact several training programs and check tuition requirements, courses of study, and future employment possibilities. All of these vary in different parts of the country. A typical course is approximately an academic year's duration, although many today are abbreviated or set to conform with the applicant's pace. These courses all include lectures on Montessori practice and theory, practical sessions, observation, use of materials, field trips, and an internship of several months. Aside from reading several Montessori books, one should also observe a few Montessori schools and speak with certified Montessorians to gain more insight into the method.

A well-known and accepted credential is offered through a correspondence course from the St. Nicholas Training Centre in London. The Centre was originally founded by Dr. Montessori, but is now operated autonomously of A.M.I. Certification is available for teaching children up through age ten. Tuition is considerably lower than full-time training courses, and a two-week "vacation course," taken in London or in various locations throughout the United States, gives the students their practical experience with the materials prior to sitting for exams. This course does not, however, include an internship for working with children in an actual classroom situation. I myself took this course many years ago, when A.M.S. and A.M.I. were still formulating their policies for American courses of study. At the time I was assisting in a Montessori classroom under the able direction and tutelage of a highly trained Montessori director and educator. I would not recommend the correspondence course unless similar circumstances were available. I feel that it's excellent, however, for parents who want to delve deeper into the intricacies of Montessori without pursuing certification, or for someone who wants to train in order to act in the capacity of aide or assistant but cannot afford the time or money required for the more intensive programs. For anyone wishing to start their own school or become a full-time directress, the more intensified course of study is, of course, preferable and recommended.

Below are selected teacher-training programs currently approved and available. Further information may be obtained by writing directly to the individual centers or consulting your local telephone directory.

AMERICAN MONTESSORI SOCIETY (A.M.S.)

CALIFORNIA

College of Notre Dame Teacher Training Program
1500 Ralston Avenue
Belmont, CA 94002

Montessori Elementary Teacher Training Center
16292 Foothill Blvd.
San Leandro, CA 94578

Montessori Western Teacher Training Program
5856 Belgrave
Garden Grove, CA 92645

St. Mary's College Montessori Teacher Training Program
Dept. of Graduate Education—Box K
Moraga, CA 94575

COLORADO

Rocky Mountain Montessori Teacher Training Program
3300 Redstone Road
Boulder, CO 80303

FLORIDA

MTTI/Montessori Teacher Training Institute
6050 S.W. Red Road
Miami, FL 33143

HAWAII

Chaminade Univeristy of Honolulu Montessori
Teacher Training Program
3140 Waialae Avenue
Honolulu, HI 96816

ILLINOIS

Meca-Seton
P.O. Box 6850, Chicago, IL 60680
or 302 S. Grant, Hinsdale, IL 60521

Midwest Montessori Teacher Training Center
1010 West Chicago Avenue
Chicago, IL 60622
or 1439 Monroe
River Forest, IL 60305

INDIANA

St. Mary of the Woods College
Montessori Teacher Education Program
St. Mary of the Woods, IN 47876

MARYLAND

The Institute for Advanced Montessori Studies
2400 Bell Pre Road
Silver Spring, MD 20906

MASSACHUSETTS

New England Montessori Teacher Education Center
P.O. Box 2826 McCormack Station
Boston, MA 02101

MICHIGAN

Michigan Montessori Center
2695 Walnut Lake Road
West Bloomfield, MI 48033

MINNESOTA

College of St. Catherine/Montessori Teacher Training Program
2004 Randolph Avenue
St. Paul, MN 55105

MISSOURI and NEBRASKA

Great Plains Montessori Teacher Training Program
12610 Pacific Street
Omaha, NE 68154

NEW YORK

Aerco Ithaca Montessori Teaching Training Program
1400 E. Willow Grove Avenue
Philadelphia, PA 19118

Buffalo Montessori Teacher Education Program
171 Countryside Lane
Williamsville, NY 14221

Center for Montessori Teacher Education
25 Roxbury Road
Scarsdale, NY 10583

Champ Montessori Teacher Training Program
311 W. 120th Street
New York, NY 10027

New York University Montessori Teacher Training Program
200 East Building, Washington Square
New York, NY 10003

NORTH CAROLINA

Center for Montessori Teacher Education
1810 White Fork Road
Raleigh, NC 27608

OHIO

Columbus Montessori Center
300 E. Main Street
Columbus, OH 43215

Xavier University Montessori Teacher Training Program
1024 Dana Avenue
Cincinnati, OH 45207

OKLAHOMA

Oklahoma City University Teacher Training Program
24th and N. Blackwelder
Oklahoma City, OK 73106

PENNSYLVANIA

Aerco Philadelphia Montessori Teacher Training Program
1400 E. Willow Grove Avenue
Philadelphia, PA 19118

Carlow College Montessori Teacher Training Center
3333 Fifth Avenue
Pittsburgh, PA 15213

Chestnut Hill College Montessori Teacher Training Program
Germantown and Northwestern Avenues
Philadelphia, PA 19118

TENNESSEE

Memphis Montessori Institute
1021 Mosby Road
Memphis, TN 38116

TEXAS

Dallas Montessori Teacher Programs
P.O. Box 2423
Dallas, TX 75221

Houston Montessori Center
2623 Kipling Street
Houston, TX 77098

VIRGINIA

Virginia Commonwealth University Montessori Teacher Training
Program
School of Education
Richmond, VA 23284

WASHINGTON

Montessori Elementary Teacher Training Center
Seattle Univeristy, School of Education
Seattle, WA 98122

MEXICO

Colegio Montessori Sierra Madre A.C. Centro de Entrenamiento
Juarez 250 sur San Pedro
Garza Garcia, N.L., Mexico

ASSOCIATION MONTESSORI INTERNATIONALE (A.M.I.)

CALIFORNIA

Montessori Education Center
3895 Nelson Drive
Palo Alto, CA 94306

Montessori Institute of Los Angeles, Inc
2918 Santa Monica Blvd-Suite D
Santa Monica, CA 90404

FLORIDA

Southern Montessori Institute
3060 Orange Street
Miami, FL 33133

GEORGIA

Montessori Institute of Atlanta
P.O. Box 52602
Atlanta, GA 30305

MISSOURI

Avila College, Education Dept.
11901 Wornall Road
Kansas City, MO 64145

Montessori Training Center of St. Louis
12318 Manchester Road
Des Peres, MO 65131

NEW JERSEY

Montessori Center of New Jersey
79 Midland Avenue
Montclair, NJ 07042

OHIO

Edgecliff College
2220 Victory Parkway
Cincinnati, OH 45206

Montessori Institute of Cleveland
2140 Lee Road
Cleveland Heights, OH 44118

WASHINGTON, DC

Washington Montessori Institute
2119 S Street NW
Washington, DC 20008

WISCONSIN

The Midwest Montessori Institute
5411 W. Lisbon Avenue
Milwaukee, WI 53210

INTERNATIONAL MONTESSORI SOCIETY (I.M.S.)

International Montessori Society
912d Thayer Avenue
Silver Spring, MD 20910
(I.M.S. offers courses in many states through a unique Independent Study program)

WORLDWIDE TEACHER TRAINING COURSES

The following is a list of selected institutions and organizations throughout the world offering Montessori teacher-training certificates.

DENMARK

Nordisk Montessori Kursus
Hellerupgardvej 13
Hellerup, Denmark

ENGLAND

St. Nicholas Training Centre
23 Princes Gate
London SW7, England

FRANCE

Centre Montessori de France
22 rue Eugene Flachat
Paris 17e, France

GERMANY

Arbeitskreis Berlin of the Deutsche Montessori Gesellschaft
Friedrich Wilhelmstrasse 72-74
Berlin-Templeof, Germany

Deutsche Montessori Gesellschaft
Fellnerstrasse 1
Frankfort, Germany

HOLLAND

Dutch Montessori Society, Secretariet
161 Koninginneweg
Amsterdam, Holland

Municipal Training Center
Nieuwe Prinsengracht 89
Amsterdam, Holland

Roman Catholic Montessori Training Centre
Oude Stadsgracht 32
Nijmegan, Holland

Roman Catholic Training Center Sint Lucia
Aert van Nesstraat
Rotterdam, Holland

INDIA

Ceylon Montessori Training Course
9 Nimalha Gardens
Kollupithya, Colombo 3, Ceylon, India

Good Shepherd Maria Montessori Training Center
Colombo 13
Ceylon, India

Montessori Training Center for Village Schools
Yeotmal, Madhya
Pradesh, India

H. RESEARCH AND THE SIX-YEAR STUDY

Truly conclusive results to determine the advantages of a Montessori education have been difficult to obtain because of the wide variety of teaching styles within Montessori. The high cost of research and the time factors involved are other aspects hampering significant research. There is a great need for more testing and research to determine the true long-range value of Montessori early education. Several tests have shown that children with some kind of educational pre-school experience show an overwhelming advantage throughout their fourteen years of schooling over those without such early training. Those with Montessori schooling are only slightly ahead of the groups with some other kind of pre-primary experience.

Possibilities for research of the method are extensive and can cover a wide range of specialties, such as: the normal child, the gifted child, emotionally, physically and mentally handicapped, culturally deprived, application of the method in day care centers, etcetera. Due to cost and lack of personnel, such studies have not been done.

In 1965, the Cincinnati Montessori Society, the Carnegie Foundation, and the Cincinnati Board of Education, begin a six-year study, using children from three different communities. Some children were from Montessori schools, while others were from traditional urban public school classrooms. This was the first scientifically designed research project to study the Montessori method of education.

The report, known as The Sands School Project Report, examined performance on several variables including self-concept, social competence, curiosity, creativity, motor impulse control, innovative behavior, and some aspects of conventional intelligence. Academic achievement, per se, was not examined. The conclusion, drawn from this research suggests, ". . . considerable promise for the Montessori approach in fostering a wide range of desirable behavior in elementary school age children."

A six-year followup program evaluated whether or not continued and early exposure to Montessori education made a difference in later academic life. Verbal and mathematic skills were measured by the Metropolitan Achievement Test (M.A.T.) in third-grade children of varied pre-school and primary school experiences. The groups studied included: (1) children with four years of Montessori pre-school and primary school education; (2) children with two years of Montessori pre-school; (3) children with one year of Head Start prior to kindergarten; and (4) children with no school experience prior to kindergarten.

I feel that the results of this test were not really conclusive enough to formulate anything more than a probable generalization. Age was a significant factor in correlating achievement, and all the children were from low socioeconomic groupings.

While the children in group (1) (four years of Montessori) achieved high scores, it was apparent that to maintain the effect of a higher level of proficiency it was necessary to continue the method of learning beyond preschool years. The groups rated in predictable pre-hypothesis fashion, i.e., children who attended Montessori pre-school will score higher than will children who attended no pre-school or attended Head Start, and children who attended pre-school will score higher than children who did not attend pre-school. Group (1) children achieved higher minimum scores overall with a large differential between the highest minimum score of the next group.

In summary, ". . . a small group of children who attended Montessori classes for at least four years beginning during preschool scored first of four groups in all seven of the M.A.T. subscores while they were in the third grade. The children were compared with children who had had Montessori pre-school, Head Start, or no preschool experience. The Montessori children scored significantly higher in Word Analysis and Math Problem-Solving, two areas considered important in the Montessori philosophy. Thus, the influence of the Montessori program on academic achievement has been shown to be strong. Age was a factor in influencing scores. A wide range of further studies is needed, but this material indicated that the Montessori approach with primary school chidren of lower SES [socioeconomic strata] was more effective than regular public school primary grade programs, regardless of the previous pre-school experience."

In a letter written in September, 1977, D. June Sciarra informed me that she and her co-worker had done no further work after their six-year study, "because we found that we no longer had enough children in the group experiencing at least four years of Montessori to be able to have any confidence in research results." Thus, what could have been a good followup for examining the long-term effects of various pre-school programs has ended until new research is begun somewhere else.

There have been no updated studies conducted to follow the progress of "Montessori students." In light of the controversies arising in the past decade as to "What is 'Montessori'?" and interpretational problems that could occur, perhaps further studies would become invalid anyway. Realistically, how can there be comparisons? Who can truly judge what is the result of Montessori and what comes from environment, heredity, and the many other component parts that blend together to create an individual? Can one ingredient actually stand alone in that amalgam?

The following are excerpts from a letter received in 1982 from a former Montessori student teacher from 1932 to 1935. The number of parallels between Montessori then and now are surprising; its enthusiastic acceptance by some and total rejection by others.

. . . The school was located on New York's West Side in the early '20's and then into a building especially built for them in 1929 or 1930.

The Children's Home School (founded in 1916 as a demonstration school) had a flight of child-size stairs (awfully difficult for us practice teachers to manage to climb, with the narrow treads and low risers) which took the children from their classroom level to the roof play level. I was a student teacher there . . . At that time it was a three-year course, although earlier, in the '20's it had been a two-year course. Throughout the course, we followed Mme. Montessori's precepts of observing children in classrooms, and slowly participating more and more in giving lessons, and ending with an eight-week period of being wholly responsible for a class, with a student assistant. There were about 8 schools, all with Montessori teachers, chiefly in Day Care Centers (called Day Nurseries in those days) mostly on the Lower East Side of New York. The Children's Home School took children from 18 months through third grade, with about 15 at each level, as I remember it. These were children from privileged families, in sharp contrast to those in the Day Care Centers, where the teachers were all graduates of Miss McLin's course. In our class there were 17 graduating teachers, and that was the general range of numbers until the early '50's when there was a falling-off. . . . Other schools were offering degrees in Early Childhood Education and charging much less for the courses. We tried various associations, first with Adelphi College on Long Island and later with New York University whereby we could be given credits for our work at the Foundation and get our B.S. in another year plus 2 summer sessions. . . . It was sad that we had to close so shortly before there was the revival of interest in Montessori's work . . . One other factor entered in to complicate our problems. To be certified by New York State a school had to meet certain standards, quite correctly. The woman who had a high position in the department of education of New York State was a follower of Kirkpatrick and the Columbia Teacher's College school of thought. She particularly was disturbed at having the children work with such small things as the cylindrical insets, which she felt unduly strained the small muscles of the young child. That the youngest children took such delight in the small cube from the pink tower that reserves had always to be kept on hand because they went home in pockets, that they loved the cylindrical insets, and many of the other small-handling materials, had no effect on her determination to put the Child Education Foundation out of business.

. . . The years I spent at the Child Education Foundation were the most influential years of my life, and yet I did not go there because they taught the Montessori method, about which I knew little or nothing beforehand, but because they believed in observing children in classrooms from the first day of the course. We also had assignments to observe children in city playgrounds, as well, I remember. The training in observation built such a habit of observation that has stood me well ever since. I am struck by new young teachers who seem to see nothing much but the curriculum syllabus they must get through . . .

I. SELECTED BIBLIOGRAPHY

BOOKS BY MARIA MONTESSORI

The Montessori Method, New York, Schocken Books, 1964. Her first book, considered to be the definitive statement of her method. Contents cover the new pedagogy in its relation to modern science, history of methods, inaugural address given at opening of "Children's House," pedagogical methods used in the "Children's House," discipline, how lessens should be given, exercises of practical life, reflection, muscular education, nature in education, manual labor, education of the senses, use of didactic materials, intellectual education, method for teaching reading and writing, description of the method and didactic materials used, language in childhood, teaching numeration, sequence of exercises, general review of discipline, conclusion and impressions.

Spontaneous Activity in Education, New York, Schocken Books, 1965. The first two volumes dealing with the advanced use of the method. Includes a survey of the child's life and of modern education, Dr. Montessori's contribution to experimental science, the preparation of the teacher, environment, attention, will, intelligence, and imagination.

The Montessori Elementary Material, Cambridge, Massachusetts, Robert Bentley, Inc., 1965. Volume Two of the advanced method. Contains detailed descriptions of grammar, arithmetic, geometry, drawing, music, metrics, and illustrations.

Dr. Montessori's Own Handbook, New York, Schocken Books, 1965. Text and illustrations act as a practical guide to the method and includes discussion of a "Children's House," the method, motor education, sensory education, language and knowledge of the world, freedom, writing, reading of music, arithmetic, and moral factors.

The Absorbent Mind, New York, Dell Publishing Co., 1967. Based on lectures given by Dr. Montessori during her first training course in India and illustrating the unique mental powers of the young child, allowing him to construct all the characteristics of the human personality in a brief period of years.

The Secret of Childhood, Notre Dame, Indiana, Fides Publishers, Inc., 1966. Shows Dr. Montessori's insight and wisdom into the nature of the child as he revealed himself to her, and her observations of him while formulating her new method of education.

The Discovery of the Child, Notre Dame, Indiana, Fides Publishers, Inc. 1967. This is a statement of the conclusions reached by Dr. Montessori after years of studying the child and establishing her method. Repetitious of earlier works.

What You Should Know About Your Child, Adyar, India, Kalakshetra Publications, 1961. An interpretation of the essence of Dr. Montessori's lectures and work by an Indian in an attempt to diffuse her ideas of the nature and soul of the child.

Education for a New World, Adyar, India, Kalakshetra Publications, 1946. A summary of earlier works dealing with the powers of the child and his task in constructing his personality in the first few years of life.

To Educate the Human Potential, Adyar, India, Kalakshetra Publications, 1948. Meant as a companion volume to follow *Education for a New World,* to help teachers understand the needs of the child after the age of six. The first few chapters are mainly psychological, the rest deal with Dr. Montessori's Cosmic Plan, which involves all unconsciously or consciously serving what she refers to as "the great purpose of life."

Reconstruction in Education, Adyar, India, Theosophical Publishing House, 1948. Statement of her works and the need to change education with emphasis on the child.

The Child in the Family, Chicago, Illinois, Henry Regnery Company, 1970. A summarization of Dr. Montessori's insights into helping the child and the adults' interpretation and treatment of him. An attempt to better answer the question, "What is the child?" and to understand his relative position in the world.

Childhood Education, Chicago, Illinois, Henry Regnery Company, 1974. Originally published as *The Formation of Man,* this deals with Maria Montessori's answers to those critics who object and misunderstand her method. Contents are: Prejudices and Nebulae, Prejudices in Science and Education, and World Illiteracy.

From Childhood to Adolescence, New York, Schocken Books, 1973. An assemblage of lectures originally translated into French and speaking to the problems of the time and the unrest and dissatisfaction in our schools and colleges. This book deals with Dr. Montessori's educational concerns for the adolescent and university student.

Education and Peace, Chicago, Henry Regnery Company, 1972. A collection of speeches presented by Dr. Montessori at international congresses and peace councils discussing her quest for a lasting peace to benefit future humanity.

[NOTE: Each of Dr. Montessori's books have, at various times, been published by several publishers. I have tried to use the most current ones and paperbacks where available.]

SELECTED BOOKS ABOUT MARIA MONTESSORI AND
THE METHOD

[NOTE: There have been many books written about Maria Montessori and the Montessori method over the years. The following is only a representative selection.]

Blessington, John P., *Let My Children Work*, Garden City, New York, Anchor Press/Doubleday, 1975. Written by the headmaster of Whitby School from 1962 to 1973, this is a tightly written book about change and education, giving practical insights on both. It also gives the reader an overview of the reintroduction of the Montessori method in the United States and Whitby's founding and growing pains.

Carinato, Sister Mary Ellen, *Montessori Matters, Cincinnati, Ohio*, Sisters of Notre Dame de Namur, 1983. A detailed lesson plan and explanation of materials and usage.

Farrow, Elvira and Hill, Carol, *Montessori on a Limited Budget*, Los Angeles, California, Education Systems Publisher, 1984. Adapting Montessori to use readily available objects and ideas.

Fisher, Dorothy Canfield, *Montessori for Parents*, rev. ed., Cambridge, Massachusetts, Robert Bentley Incorporated, 1965. The first book written for the lay person in the early ninteen hundreds. Gives a general view of the method at that time and introduces it to parents.

Fisher, Dorothy Canfield, *The Montessori Manual for Teachers and Parents*, rev. ed., Cambridge, Massachusetts, Robert Bentley Incorporated, 1964. Written for use by teachers and parents without Montessori training. The chapters are: 1. Something Wrong With Modern Education, 2. Dr. Montessori to the Rescue, 3. An Italian Casa dei Bambini, 4. Use of the Apparatus With Comprehensive and Practical Directions to the Mother or Teacher, 5. A Suggestive Exercise on Nature Study, 6. Montessori General Ideas About Discipline and Obedience, 7. Questions Answered for Mother and Teacher.

Fleege, Virginia. *Montessori Index*, Montessori Publications, River Forest, IL, 1974. A complete index of Montessori and Montessori related books.

Gitter, Lena L. *The Montessori Way*, Seattle, Washington, Special Child Publications, Incorporated, 1970. A practical guide for using Montessori's ideas and philosophy in working with the special child.

Gitter, Lena, *The Montessori Approach to Special Education*, Johnson, Pennsylvania, Mafex Associates, Inc., 1971. For use in adapting Montessori methods to those with special needs.

Hainstock, Elizabeth G., *Teaching Montessori in the Home: The Pre-School Years*, New York, New American Library, Plume Books, 1976. The first layman's guide introducing the use of the Montessori method in the home and giving simple instructions on making the materials and adapting classroom exercises to home use for the pre-school child. Step-by-step exercises. (Originally published in 1968 by Random House, New York.)

Hainstock, Elizabeth G., *Teaching Montessori in the Home: The School Years*, New York, New American Library, Plume Books, 1978. The companion volume to *Teaching Montessori in the Home: The Pre-School Years*. Deals with the child of school age and gives specific exercises for supplementing and aiding school work. (Originally published in 1971 by Random House, New York.)

Kramer, Rita, *Maria Montessori: A Biography*, New York, G.P. Putnam's Sons, 1976. The first definitive biography of Maria Montessori, tracing the woman, the myth, the method and the movement through extensive research and interviews. Gives much insight into her as a person and an educator.

Lillard, Paula Polk, *Montessori: A Modern Approach*, New York, Schocken Books, 1972. Deals with an historical introduction to Montessori, the philosophy, the method, Montessori and parents, the approach to writing and reading, and a discussion of Montessori today.

Malloy, Terry, *Montessori and Your Child*, Schocken Books, 1974. A brief and simplified discussion of the child's needs and how his parents can help him through the Montessori method.

Montessori Mario, M., Jr., *Education for Human Development*, New York, Schocken Books, 1976. Maria Montessori's grandson discusses her views of education as a necessity in the formation of the human personality and the relationship of man to the cosmos, as related to problems and opportunities of the modern world.

Orem R.C., Editor, *A Montessori Handbook*, New York, G.P. Putnam's Sons, 1965. Edited to integrate Dr. Montessori's own writings with more up-to-date Montessori's theories and practices in the United States.

Orem, R.C., Editor, *Montessori and the Special Child*, New York, G.P. Putnam's Sons, 1969. An application of Montessori's principles to educating the handicapped, the disadvantaged and other children who are out of the norm. Written by experienced contributors.

Orem, R.C., Editor, *Montessori for the Disadvantaged*, New York, G.P. Putnam's Sons, 1968. Contributions by persons dealing with the application of Montessori's educational principles to the war on poverty.

Orem, R.C., Editor, *Maria Montessori: Methods, Schools and Materials, As Described in the Famous McClure's Magazine Articles*, Alvin, Texas, George Chyka Productions, 1978. Concerns the roots of Montessori and its introduction to America, through early magazine articles.

Rambusch, Nancy McCormick, *Learning How to Learn: An American Approach to Montessori*, Baltimore, Maryland, Helicon Press,

1962. The book that heralded the revival of the Montessori method in the United States. Gives an analysis of contemporary education and the Montessori approach to early education.

Standing, E.M., *Maria Montessori: Her Life and Work*, rev. ed., New York, New American Library, 1984. Written by a loving friend and disciple of Dr. Montessori's, giving a detailed discussion of her life, her work, and her method.

Standing, E.M., *The Montessori Revolution in Education*, New York, Schocken Books, 1966. A systematic presentation of the method, covering the principles and application, with illustrations and a discussion of Montessori in America and its possibilities for the future.

Wolf, Aline D. *A Parent's Guide to the Montessori Classroom*, Altoona, Pennsylvania, Parent Child Press, 1980. Pictures and descriptions of the materials.

J. SOME HIGHLIGHTS IN THE LIFE OF MARIA MONTESSORI

1896 Became the first woman to receive her doctorate in medicine, University of Rome
1898 Director of the Orthophrenic Institute, Rome
1904 Lecturer in Anthropology, University of Rome
1907 Opening of the first Casa dei Bambini
1909 Publication of *The Montessori Method*
1911 Opening of the first Montessori school in the United States
1911 Articles in *McClure's Magazine*, United States
1913 Model Montessori classroom set up in London
     Montessori's first trip to the United States
     First Montessori school established in Spain
1914 Publication of *Dr. Montessori's Own Handbook*
     Second International Montessori Congress, Rome
     Opening of first Casa dei Bambini, Holland
1915 Third International Training Course, San Francisco
     Second trip to the United States
     Model classroom at San Francisco Exposition

1916 Publication of *The Advanced Montessori Method*
1917 Lecture to Pedagogical Society of Amsterdam
1919 First International Training Course, London
1920 Lectures at the University of Amsterdam
1922 Lecture in Berlin
1924 International Training Course, Amsterdam
1926 Speaker at League of Nations, Geneva
      Lectures in Berlin
      Formation of Montessori Society, India
      Private audience with Mussolini
      Made honorary member of the Fascist Women's Organization
1927 Montessori Society of Argentine
      Establishment of Training School, Rome
      Travels to England
1929 First International Congress, Denmark
      Founding of Association Montessori International (A.M.I.)
1930 Formation of A.M.I. branch, England
1932 Second International Montessori Congress, Nice
      Publication of *Peace in Education*
1933 International course, Barcelona
1934 Montessori Congress, Ireland
      Formation of Montessori Society, Ireland
1936 Publication of *The Child in the Family* and *The Secret of Childhood*
      Amsterdam became A.M.I. Headquarters
      Montessori established her home in Laren, Holland
      Fifth Montessori Congress, Oxford
1937 Left Spain
      Sixth International Montessori Congress, Copenhagen
1938 Seventh International Montessori Congress, Edinburgh
1939 Speech to World Fellowship of Faith
      Montessori goes to India
1945 First All-India Montessori Congress, Jaipur
1946 Returns to Holland from India
      Courses in London and Scotland
      Publication of *Education for a New World*
1947 Reestablishment of Opera Montessori, Italy
      Celebrates 40th anniversary of Casa dei Bambini
      Establishment of Montessori Centre, London
      Returns to India

1948 Publication of *Discovery of the Child*, *To Educate the Human Potential*, and *What You Should Know About Your Child*

1949 Receives Cross of the Legion of Honor, France
Eighth International Congress, San Remo
To Pakistan to found a Montessori Assocation
Publication of *The Absorbent Mind*

1950 Nominated for Nobel Peace Prize
Delegate to UNESCO Conference, Florence
Publication of *The Formation of Man*

1951 Ninth International Montessori Congress, London

1952 Maria Montessori dies, May 6, 1952